no. 99

Gluten-free Cookery

Hodder & Stoughton

A MEMBER OF THE HODDER HEADLINE GROUP

With thanks to all our friends and members of the Coeliac Society
who have tested, tasted and contributed ideas for recipes.

Orders: Please contact Bookpoint Ltd, 130 Milton Park, Abingdon,
Oxon OX14 4SB. Telephone (44) 01235 400414. Fax: (44) 01235 400454.
Lines are open from 9 am–6 pm Monday to Saturday, with a 24-hour
message answering service. Email address: orders@bookpoint.co.uk

British Library Cataloguing in Publication Data
Thomson, Peter
   Gluten-free Cookery: Complete Guide
   I. Title
   641.5632

ISBN 0340 78924 7

First published 1995. This edition published 2001.
Impression number   8 7 6 5 4 3 2
Year   2004 2003 2002 2001

Typeset by Fakenham Photosetting Limited
Printed in Great Britain for Hodder & Stoughton Educational,
a division of Hodder Headline Plc, 338 Euston Road, London NW1 3BH
by The Bath Press Ltd

Contents

Food from plants   1

Dairy products   30

Meat   32

Fish and other Seafood   34

Other ingredients   37

Forbidden: Food ingredients to avoid   39
Equipment   40

SECTION 2: RECIPES   42

Gluten-free flour mixes   42

Recipes for feeding children   44

Breakfasts   48

Lunch and snack dishes   54

Starters   65

Soups   67

Meat and poultry   75

Sausages   89

Fish   92

Bread   97

Crispbreads   109

Pancakes   113

Scones   117

Cakes and buns   119

Christmas and party   136

Biscuits   140

Puddings   151

Pastry   165

Salads   169

Vegetables   170

Vegetarian dishes   178

Sauces   183

Jelly and Jam   191

Pickles   193

Home-made Sweets   194

SECTION 1: INGREDIENTS

Food from plants

Do not use wheat flour, wholemeal flour, oatmeal, rye flour, strong flour, semolina, barley flour, self-raising flour, spelt flour, triticale (a hybrid wheat), couscous.
Do not use products made from these flours, such as semolina.
Do not use pastas, such as spaghetti, macaroni, lasagne.
Do not use products that are just labelled starch, food starch, edible starch or modified starch.
Beware of any products that may use starch as a filler, such as mustard powder and white pepper.
Beware of any products that contain unspecified sweeteners and stabilisers. These may be chemically modified wheat flour.

Agar Agar
A thickening agent made from seaweed. It dissolves in hot water to form a liquid that sets when it is cold.

Alfalfa (Medicago sativa)
The tiny seeds of this plant are sprouted and used in salads or casseroles. The sprouted seeds contain 20 per cent protein, vitamins C and B_{12} and small amounts of other vitamins and minerals.

Allspice (Pimenta dioica)
Allspice is ground from sun-dried berries of a tropical evergreen tree. It is best purchased as the whole dried spice and ground immediately before use. It is used in marinades, pickles, mulled wine and to flavour both sweet and savoury dishes. It was originally used by the Mayans as a flavouring with chocolate.

Almond (Prunus dulcis, var. Dulcis)
The sweet almond produces a nut inside a hard shell. The nut is eaten whole or ground into a flour for use in baking and confectionery. The

1

almond has 17 per cent protein, 54 per cent oil and high levels of calcium and other minerals, as well as vitamins from the E and B groups. Large amounts of almond (more than 8 oz) should not be eaten in one sitting. It should not be confused with the nut of the bitter almond, which is poisonous.

Amaranth (Amaranthus leucocarpus, Amaranthus caudatus, Amaranthus cruentus)

Amaranth has been cultivated in Mexico for over 7000 years. The Aztec civilisation stored over 20 000 tons of the grain, keeping it for two to ten years as a reserve against times of famine. It is now grown in northern India and Nepal as well as Mexico, Guatemala and Peru. Most of the grain in English shops comes from the USA.

Amaranth is 15 per cent protein, 7 per cent fat and 63 per cent carbohydrate. It has good lycine and calcium levels. It is also easily digested.

It adds a good flavour but does not stick together well when cooked on its own, therefore it should be used to make cakes, biscuits and pancakes in combination with other flours.

Amaranth flour does not keep well unless it is stored in the deep-freeze. It is best purchased as grain and put through a grain mill just before use.

Amaranth can be grown in a frost-free garden where it forms bold red spikes of flowers up to 1 m high. It must be started early in the spring if it is to produce a good crop of grain. When threshed, by rubbing the ripe seed from the seed heads, a small husk remains mixed with the seed and this is best removed by sieving.

Amaranth spinach (Amaranthus tricolor)

A highly nutritious leafy vegetable which should only be cooked briefly by steaming or stir-frying. It is much richer in vitamins, especially vitamin A, than cabbage or lettuce.

Aniseed (Pimpinella anisum)

Aniseed or anise are the small seeds of a tender annual that is a native of the eastern Mediterranean countries. The seed should be grey-green when purchased, going grey when stale. It should be ground immediately before use. It can be used to flavour bread, cakes and biscuits as well as drinks and sweets.

Anise, Star (Illicium verum)

The seeds of this tree are used ground into a spice in many savoury dishes of China and South East Asia.

Annatto (Bixa orellana)

Annatto is the red seed of a tropical shrub. It has a slightly sweet, peppery taste but is mostly used to give its colour to the food. The seeds can be fried gently in oil for one minute. One teaspoon (5 ml) of seeds is enough for most dishes. The seeds are then discarded and the oil used. A few seeds can also be boiled with rice, or used to colour a stock.

Apple (Malus spp.)

Fruit of a hardy tree, fresh or dried apple can be used as an ingredient in baking where it imparts a moist texture and helps to bind the dough together. Apple mixes well with other fruits in sweet dishes.

Apricot (Prunus armenaica)

These fruit are rich in vitamin A, iron and potassium. The dried fruit can be eaten raw or used in cakes, or reconstituted by soaking in water.

Hunza dried apricots are whole sun-dried apricots with the stone still inside.

Sulphurated dried apricots are a bright orange but the untreated dried fruit are darker in colour. Bright and shiny dried fruit may have been treated with the mineral oil, liquid paraffin. All dried fruit should be stored in a cool dry place.

Apricot jam goes well with pastry or cakes.

Arrowroot (Maranta arundinacea)

This is a fine grained starch prepared from the rhizomes of the herbaceous tropical perennial. It is easily digested and is excellent for thickening sauces. The sauce should not be overcooked.

Artichoke – Globe (Cynara scolymus)

The flower-heads of this herbaceous perennial can be boiled, baked or fried. The fleshy base of the scales and the base of the flower are the parts that are eaten.

Artichoke – Jerusalem (Helianthus tuberosus)

The tubers of this sunflower are eaten boiled, baked or fried. They have an unusually sweet flavour from the sugar called inulin that they contain, but this can cause indigestion.

Asparagus (Asparagus officinalis)

The young shoots are cooked by poaching in the minimum quantity of water and served with butter. Their flavour is easily overwhelmed by any other sauce.

Aubergine (Solanum melongena)

This fruit is always cooked as a vegetable. The fruit should be shiny, firm and heavy. There is a tendency towards bitterness which can be removed by rolling slices in salt and then leaving to stand for half an hour. The salt should then be washed off before use.

Aubergines mix well with onion, tomato, garlic and olive oil. They can be sliced and fried, baked or stuffed with savoury mixtures.

Avocado (Persea americana)

This is the fruit of a tropical tree. It is unusual in that the fruit does not start to ripen until it is picked. Buy avocados rock hard several days before use and ripen on a warm shelf. The fruit is 15 per cent fat but contains no cholesterol. It is also rich in vitamins E, B_6 and folic acid, has good levels of vitamin C and potassium and supplies other B vitamins and minerals. Avocado is best eaten raw, mixed with shellfish, fish, citrus fruit, eggs or salads. It can also be added to soups at the end of cooking.

Azuki Bean, Aduki (Phaseolus angularis)

These beans are used to make sweet fillings for pies, buns and pastries. They should be cooked by boiling in slightly salted water. They are a good source of protein, iron and B group vitamins.

Banana (Musa spp.)

The fruit of this giant herbaceous plant are easily digested and have a high nutritional value, with good levels of vitamin C, B_6, folic acid and potassium.

Banana flour is produced by freeze-drying puréed banana. It is a very fine powder with a low density. It is very useful for its moisture-absorbing and holding properties, making pancakes, bread, scones and cakes much moister, lighter and more open in texture. It should not be used in greater proportions than of a quarter flour mixture as, on its own, it produces a sticky banana paste. If you cannot obtain banana flour, put dried banana chips through a liquidiser. This produces a coarser flour but it is just as useful. Fresh banana can be substituted by using double the weight of the dried banana and reducing the quantity of any added liquid.

Banana chips may have added coconut oil, honey and sugar.

Basil (Ocinum basilicum)

A herb used to flavour savoury dishes. The young fresh leaves have the best flavour.

Bay leaves (Laurus nobilis)

Bay leaves are picked from the hardy shrub and can be used fresh or dried when they should still retain their green colour. They are used to flavour soups, stews, casseroles, marinades and pickles as well as fish and meat dishes.

Beans

Most beans are an excellent source of protein, calcium, iron and vitamins B_1 and niacin. Dried beans contain no vitamin C but this is produced by the process of sprouting. Good sprouting beans are aduki, whole lentils, mung beans and chick peas.

Beans should never be eaten raw because they contain poisons that are destroyed by soaking and cooking.

BLACK-EYE BEAN, COW PEA, KAFIR-BEAN, YARD BEAN (Vigna unguiculata)
These are quick to cook with a creamy texture. They contain 23 per cent protein and are an excellent source of iron and vitamins B_2, B_1 and niacin.

SCARLET RUNNER BEAN (Phaseolus coccineus)
A vigorous climber. The fresh bean pods should be picked before they have reached full size.

BUTTER BEAN OR LIMA BEAN (Phaseolus lunatus)
The dried bean should be soaked overnight before use. Cook by

simmering until tender. This bean is good with strong flavoured dishes. The beans contain 20 per cent protein and are a good source of calcium, iron, vitamins A, niacin, B_1 and a small amount of vitamin C.

MUNG BEAN OR GREEN GRAM **(Phaseolus aureus or Vigna radiata)**
These have the highest vitamin A content of any bean. They contain 24 per cent protein and are a rich source of iron, calcium and the vitamins B_1, niacin, B_2 and in the sprouted bean vitamin C. They are excellent ground to produce Gram flour, germinated in the dark to produce bean sprouts or used whole in soups and stews. They are a very easily digested bean.

FRENCH, KIDNEY, HARICOT BEANS **(Phaseolus vulgaris)**
The dried ripe seeds can be stored for long periods. They should be soaked in water overnight before cooking by boiling vigorously for ten minutes and then simmering until tender when they can be added to a sauce or meat dish. They are an excellent source of protein, iron, potassium, zinc and B vitamins.

Fresh bean pods should be picked before they have grown to their full size.

BROAD BEAN **(Vicia faba)**
One of the hardiest bean crops, it is picked when almost fully grown and the beans shelled from the pods.

Beetroot (Beta vulgaris)

This beet should not be cut before boiling. It is peeled when soft and eaten hot or cold, with vinegar or a sauce. It is also used puréed in soups.

Bilberry and Cranberry (Vaccinum spp.)

These fruit make excellent jelly for serving with meat or for flavouring natural yogurt or fromage frais.

Blackcurrants and Redcurrants (Ribes spp.)

These easily grown fruit freeze well and are an excellent source of vitamin C and some iron. They can be eaten in puddings or pies or slightly stewed until just soft and served with yogurt or fromage frais. They also make a richly coloured fruit wine or vitamin-rich preserves.

Borage (Borago officinalis)

The leaves and blue flowers of this hardy annual can be eaten in salads or used to flavour drinks.

Brambles, Blackberry (Rubus spp.)

This hedgerow fruit is rich in vitamins C and E with smaller quantities of other vitamins and minerals. It makes excellent jelly and wines. It does well with apple in puddings and pies It also freezes well.

Brassicas – Cabbage, Cauliflower, Sprouts, Kohlrabi, Pak Choi, Pe-Tsai

A very versatile group of vegetables that can be eaten raw as salads, cooked in soups and stews or served as a separate vegetable dish. It is important that all brassicas are cooked until just tender. More prolonged cooking destroys the texture and the nutritional value. Only pickled cabbages benefit from braising.

Brazil Nuts (Bertholletia exelsa)

Fruit of a large tropical forest tree. The kernels contain 66 per cent fat and 14 per cent protein and are highly nutritious with high levels of vitamins E and B and a range of minerals including potassium, calcium, magnesium, and iron.

Breadfruit (Artocarpus altilis)

The flesh of these large fruit is used before it is fully ripe when it is white, firm and starchy. It is served mashed and sweetened or cut in slices and baked or toasted. The seeds can be toasted. It is an excellent source of vitamin C and contains other vitamins and minerals.

Buckwheat and buckwheat flake and flour, Kasha (Fagopyrum sagittatum)

These are the fruit of a herbaceous plant native to north-eastern Europe. A husk is removed from the kernel before sale. The kernels can be cooked in a similar way to rice or used as a flour for general baking. Traditional buckwheat dishes include breakfast porridge, pancakes and a mixture with meat to form sausages.

Buckwheat contains 8–10 per cent protein and is a good source of B vitamins and minerals. Buckwheat flour has a very strong flavour and some people find it difficult to digest.

Capers (Capparis spinosa)

Capers are the small flower buds of a Mediterranean shrub. These are often preserved by pickling in salt vinegar or dry salting. They are commonly used in cold sauces with fish and salads but also occasionally with hot meat or pizza.

Carambola, Star fruit (Averrhoa carambola)

These yellow fruit come from a tropical Indonesian tree. They are sliced and used to decorate fruit salads and ice-cream. The flavour can vary from sweet to tart. They are an excellent source of vitamin C.

Caraway (Carum carvi)

Caraway is the small seed of a hardy annual plant. It should be obtained as the whole seed and if required ground this should be done immediately before use. It can be used to flavour bread, cakes and fruit, salads and vegetable dishes as well as fatty meat dishes. Caraway leaves can also be added to salads.

Cardamom (Elettaria cardamomum)

Cardamom is the seed of a tropical member of the ginger family. It retains the best flavour if obtained as whole pods which can be used whole, or the seeds can be ground when required. It can be used in cakes and pastries but features more in rice and pulse dishes as well as pickles and punches. It is also used to flavour coffee.

Carob flour (Ceratonia siliqua)

Carob flour is prepared by grinding the ripe dried pod of the Carob tree. The beans are not used.

The pods should be ground coarsely and then gently roasted after which they should be ground to a fine powder.

The pods can be chewed raw. The flour is used in cakes and biscuits or to make drinks, desserts and sweets.

Carob flour contains 8 per cent protein, 2 per cent fat, 47 per cent sugars and is a good source of many minerals including calcium, magnesium and potassium and the vitamins A, B_1, B_2 and B_5.

Cashew (Anacardium occidentale)

These nuts are roasted and then shelled by hand before sale. They contain 45 per cent fat and 20 per cent protein and are a good source of iron and calcium and vitamins E and B. They can be eaten as snacks, make excellent nut bread and are a useful component of gluten-free muesli.

Carrot (Daucus carrota)

Carrots are among the most nutritious of the hardy root crops. They have high vitamin A content and the sugar level gives them a sweet taste. They can be eaten raw as a snack or salad, or cooked in soups and stews. When cooked as a vegetable use the minimum amount of water and simmer until just tender. Grated carrot can be added to bread and cakes where it improves the texture.

Cassava (Manihot utilissima)

The coarse white flour produced from these tropical roots has some good baking qualities and can be used to make very thin crepes. See Tapioca.

Cayenne pepper and Chilli (Capsicum frutescens spp.)

Cayenne and chilli are both prepared by blending powder from the seeds and pods of a number of different types of chilli. The ripe pods should be roasted until dry and dark and then ground finely. The powder should be used sparingly with fish and other seafood dishes, savoury egg dishes, stews, casseroles and hot sauces. Fresh chilli should be only eaten in small amounts and with great care. Paprika is a slightly milder form of these peppers.

Celery (Apium graveolens var. dulce)

Celery stalks are best eaten raw with a savoury dip. They can also be used to flavour soups or cooked as a vegetable by baking or braising.

Celeriac (Apium graveolens var. rapaceum)

The swollen stem base provides a celery flavour in soups and stews or grated in salad.

Cherry, Morello (Prunus acida)

This cherry tree fruits reliably in cold temperate climates. The fruit needs to be cooked to make fruit pies and jams.

Cherry, Sweet (Prunus avium vars.)

The fruit of this hardy tree is excellent raw and adds colour to fruit salads and cold sweets. Glacé cherries are added to cakes. Maraschino cherries are preserved in almond oil.

Chervil (Anthriscus cerefolium)

The finely cut leaves of this hardy biennial herb are used to flavour soups, salads and omelettes.

Sweet chestnut flour (Castanea sativa)

The sweet chestnut is a large tree, native of southern Europe. The chestnuts contain only 2 per cent protein but have the highest sugar content of any nuts. They are a good source of potassium, calcium and magnesium and have small amounts of B group vitamins. The nuts can be roasted or boiled and eaten whole or ground into flour and used in soups, stews, pancakes, bread and cakes. Tinned pureé is an excellent substitute for the flour. If the nuts are very dry they should be soaked overnight before use.

This flour is often available in French supermarkets, but rarely in the UK.

Chick Pea, Bengal Gram, Besan flour, Garbanzo (Cicer arietinum)

This is a major Indian crop. The dried seeds should be soaked overnight before cooking. They are used to produce the dish dhal. They have a 20 per cent protein content and are an excellent source of iron, calcium, vitamins A, B_1, B_2, niacin and vitamin C.

Citrus fruit, Orange, Lemon, Tangerine, Grapefruit and Lime

All these fruit come from trees in the warm temperate or sub-tropics. They are a valuable source of vitamin C at all times of the year. Both the outer peel and the fruit make excellent flavourings for both sweet and savoury dishes.

Cinnamon (Cinnamomum zeylanicum)

Cinnamon is prepared by drying the inner bark of a tropical evergreen tree, a native of Sri Lanka. The strips of bark curl up to form quills and in this form can be used in mulled wine. It is difficult to grind and is best purchased as a powder for flavouring cakes, biscuits, fruit and for rice and curries.

Cloves (Eugenia caryophyllus)

Cloves are the young flower buds of this tropical tree, a native of the Moluccas. They are best obtained as the dried whole bud. The head of the bud is easily crumbled between the fingers if a powder is needed. One clove is often sufficient for a dish, except when decorating ham and pork. Cloves are used to flavour cakes, puddings and fruit, marinades and mulled wine, casseroles, gravies and pickles.

Cocoa (Theobroma cacao)

Cocoa is produced from the seeds of a small tree that grows in the tropical rain forests. The ripe seeds are left in heaps to ferment for a week before being dried, roasted and then ground to produce cocoa mass. Cocoa powder is produced from the cocoa mass by removing some of the cocoa butter. Bitter chocolate is produced by adding extra cocoa butter. As well as being used in drinks and sweets, cocoa is used in bread, cakes and in stews.

Coconut (Cocos nucifera)

Coconut is one of the largest seeds known, produced by a tropical palm tree. A thick layer of hard fibre surrounds the hard shelled nut and is removed before the nut is exported. The liquid inside the nut can be poured out after one of the eyes has been pierced. The flesh can be scraped out after the nut has been broken open.

Coconut milk is prepared by mixing equal quantities of shredded flesh and hot water and kneading them together. The milk is then separated out through a sieve. Some force is necessary to extract all the liquid. The liquid inside the coconut can also be used in place of water to make coconut milk. The milk is used to thicken curries and rice dishes and can be used as a replacement for dairy milk in desserts. Coconut can be used with fish as well as bread, cakes and sweets.

Coconut when fresh contains 4 per cent protein, 38 per cent fat, 11 per cent carbohydrate, 4 per cent fibre, 1 per cent minerals and small amounts of vitamins B_1, B_2, B_5 and C. Dried coconut contains 62 per cent fat and 5.5 per cent protein. It is a good source of calcium, magnesium and iron. If dried coconut seems moist when purchased it may contain additives such as propylene glycol.

Coriander (Coriandrum sativum)

Coriander is the seed of a hardy annual plant. It should be obtained as whole seeds and may be roasted slightly before use. The leaves can also be used fresh in salads but are an acquired taste. Coriander seed is a major ingredient of curry powder and is also used in stews, soups, and pickling as well as in bread and cakes.

Coffee (Coffea arabica)

The beans of this small tropical tree are fermented for a short time in water and then sun-dried. The beans are then roasted before use. Coffee flavourings are best made by boiling the beans in water for up to an hour.

Cornflour, Corn meal

See the entry under Maize.

Cucumber (Cucumis sativus)

These are the fruit of a tender trailing annual. They have a good vitamin content especially when eaten raw, sliced with a salad or chopped with yogurt. They can also be served fried or boiled with a sauce. The small cucumbers grown for pickling are often bitter when fresh.

Cumin (Cuminum cyminum)

The strongly flavoured seed of this herbaceous perennial should be roasted before use in curry, chutney and pickles.

Dates (Phoenix dactylifera)

The date palm has been in cultivation for at least 5000 years. The fruit has a high sugar content and dries and stores well. It also contains some calcium and some iron. Dried dates can be eaten as a snack or stewed with apple or other dried fruit in puddings and pies. Finely chopped dates will improve the texture of bread or cakes and can be used to replace part of the sugar content in a recipe.

Dill (Anethum graveolens)

The stalks, leaf and seeds of dill are used. This is a hardy annual plant native to southern Europe. Dill is often used in pickles and for fish sauces and herb soups. The seed can be sprinkled on bread and cakes. Unopened flower-heads can be eaten in salads.

Elder (Sambucus nigra)

The vitamin-rich fruit of this small tree makes excellent wine and jelly, and can be used to add flavour to apple and gooseberry dishes.

Endive (Cichorium endivia)

The leaves of this salad plant must be grown in darkness to prevent the development of a very bitter taste.

Fennel (Foeniculum vulgare)

Fennel is a vigorous hardy herbaceous perennial. Young leaves can be used in salads and fish sauces. The seeds are used to flavour bread, cakes and pastries and grilled fish.

Fenugreek (Trigonella foenum-graecum)

The seeds or leaves of this hairy annual are used in curry powders and to flavour dhal. The seeds are roasted lightly before grinding into a powder.

Fig (Ficus carica)

These highly nutritious fruit come from a tree of warm temperate regions. They have the highest protein content of all dried fruits and contain some calcium and iron. Fresh figs, eaten raw, have the best flavour but do not travel well. Dried figs vary in flavour and texture according to their origin. These can be eaten as a snack or soaked in water and simmered to soften them. Chopped figs can also be added to cakes and puddings.

Garlic (Allium sativum)

Garlic is the bulb of a hardy perennial. It is best used fresh, crushed through a garlic press or mashed with a little salt using a fork on a hard surface. Small amounts can be used in most meat, fish and vegetable dishes, as well as more strongly flavoured sauces and butters.

Ginger (Zingiber officinale)

Ginger is the tuberous root of a reed-like tropical herbaceous perennial. Fresh ginger has the best flavour and can be sliced or chopped finely. Dried ginger has to be well crushed with a mallet before use – it is easier to use powdered ginger. It can be used in most savoury dishes as well as in cakes and biscuits and with fruit. It is also an ingredient of curry powders and pickling spices.

Gooseberries (Ribes grossularia)

The fruit of this easy-to-grow, hardy bush varies in colour from yellow to red. They can be used in fruit stews and puddings and pies, mixing well with other fruit or with ginger. They are a rich source of vitamin C and many other vitamins and minerals.

Gram

The flour made from any pea. Some mills grind both wheat flour and pea flour in the same mill and this can result in a contamination of the flour. Gram flour is easy to produce from the whole grain in a domestic grain mill.

Grapes (Vitis vinifera)

Fresh grapes are available for most of the year. They also make excellent decorations for cakes and puddings. Dried grapes in the form of raisins, sultanas and currants can be used in a wide variety of sweet and savoury dishes or added to cold snacks. They contain some iron, calcium, phosphorus and potassium.

Guava (Psidium guajava)

The fruit of this tropical tree turn from green to yellow when ripe. They have very high values of vitamin C with smaller quantities of other vitamins and minerals. They are best stewed or made into jam or jelly.

Hazelnut (Corylus avellana)

The nut from a small bush or tree, these can be eaten fresh or lightly roasted. They can be used in cakes and sweets. They contain 36 per cent oil and 7.5 per cent protein and are good sources of calcium, magnesium, vitamin E, folacin and pantothenic acid. They also contain small amounts of iron and zinc.

Honey

Although this is collected by bees it is essentially sugars produced in the nectars of plants. Honey is said to contain the vitamins B_1, B_2, B_3, pantothenic acid, B_6, biotin and folic acid as well as a wide range of minerals.

Horseradish (Armoracia rusticana)

Horseradish is the swollen root of an easily grown hardy perennial. The fresh root is grated and can be frozen until required. It is used to make a variety of sauces to accompany meat and fish.

Kiwi Fruit (Actinidia chinensis)

The whole fruit of this semi-hardy vine is eaten raw or used to decorate cold sweets. It is a good source of vitamin C and other vitamins and minerals.

Leek (Allium ampeloprasum var. porrum)

This extremely hardy winter vegetable can be used in soups and stews or boiled in water or wine and served with a sauce.

Lentil (Lens culinaris)

The lentil has been cultivated in the Mediterranean region since ancient times. The dried seeds are used in soups and stews and can be ground to a flour for general baking purposes. Lentils are easily digested, rich in protein, iron, zinc, and have good levels of potassium and B group vitamins. Red lentils cook faster and are more easily digested than the larger green lentils.

Lettuce (Lactuca sativa)

This green salad is a useful source of vitamin A. Although mostly eaten raw, lettuce can be cooked in soups or served as a hot vegetable.

Lime (Citrus aurantifolia)

The fruit of this tropical tree are an excellent source of vitamin C. Their juice can be added to flavour many sweet or savoury dishes or used as a drink. They make an excellent marinade for fish.

Lovage (Levisticum officinale)

The stalk and leaves of this Mediterranean herb are used to flavour soups and salads.

Loquat (Eriobotrya japonica)

This semi-hardy tree produces small clusters of pear-like fruits which ripen in late spring and early summer. The fruit can be eaten fresh or used to make jelly.

Lychee Litchi (Litchi chinensis)

This evergreen tree of warm temperate regions produces a small fruit of translucent jelly in a papery skin. The large seed is not edible. The lychee is a good source of vitamin C.

Mace (Myristica fragrans)

Mace is the powdered covering of the nutmeg seed. It does not keep well so should be purchased in small quantities. It can be added in very small amounts to both sweet and savoury dishes, particularly creamed soups, casseroles and milk puddings.

Maize, Corn meal (Zea mays)

This cereal was originally cultivated in the Americas but is now a staple crop worldwide in all but the coldest regions. Different strains are grown for use as a vegetable, for making pop-corn and for flour. White maize flour can be included in most flour mixtures for bread or cakes. The finest flour is called cornflour. In the UK this is always pure maize starch but in other countries may include some wheat flour.

Maize is mostly starch, 3.5 per cent fat and a source of iron, and the yellow forms contain the pigment carotene, a precursor of vitamin A. Maize is deficient in most other nutrients. The ripe grains of maize are treated by boiling in a 5 per cent lime solution. This helps remove the gelatinous hulls which must be washed away together with the lime solution before being ground into flour. This treatment also helps to improve its nutritional value.

The freshly treated and ground moist flour is used in Mexico to produce tortillas. These are much harder to make from dry flour. Masa harina is a dry powder made from this treated maize and can be used to make tortillas.

Polenta is a partly cooked maize meal. Corn oil is 56 per cent unsaturated fat.

Mango (Mangifera indica)

The fruit of this medium-sized tropical tree is grown in all tropical countries. The skin and stone are not eaten but the sticky flesh is usually eaten raw although it can be made into jam. Unripe fruits can be made into chutney. The fruit turns from green to yellow and orange or pink as it ripens.

Maple syrup (Acer saccharum)

The concentrated sap of the sugar maple is used to make sweets, puddings and is excellent on pancakes. It contains small amounts of the vitamins B_2, B_5, and B_6 and is a good source of calcium and potassium.

Marrows, Squashes, Pumpkins (Cucurbita spp.)

The large fruits of these trailing and climbing tender annuals keep well in cool, dry conditions. They can be baked, boiled or fried, stuffed with meat or vegetables or served on their own. Young marrows, known as courgettes, should only be cooked until just tender. The grated flesh of all of these can be included in bread or cakes to improve the texture. Winter squashes have the highest food value. Pumpkin can be cooked as a dessert or made into jam. Pumpkin seeds are rich in fat and protein and can be eaten raw or deep-fried in oil.

Melons (Cucumis melo)

Melon fruits vary widely in taste, shape, texture and colour. All need warm conditions to grow. For the best flavour a melon should be ripe. Melon is generally served cold with the seeds removed. Try serving with a little ginger wine.

Millet and millet flake and flour: Bajri (Common millet, Panicum miliaceum, Red millet, Eleusine coracana, Bulrush millet, Pennisetum typhoideum)

Millet describes a group of cereals with small round seeds. They are drought resistant temperate and tropical crops that grow well in poor soils. The grain stores extremely well and has 10 per cent protein, the highest iron level of any cereal, and is an excellent source of potassium and magnesium. It also contains niacin and small amounts of B group vitamins.

In Africa the grain is often ground to a flour and used to make a porridge. The flour can be used as part of a mixture of flour to make breads. The grain can also be cooked whole in the same way as rice but it absorbs far more water. Use four or more measures of water to one measure of millet. It should be boiled for about 40 minutes.

Millet flakes are precooked by steaming before being flattened and are much quicker to use. The larger green grained millets are better to eat than the small yellow grained millet.

Mint (Mentha spp.)

There are many varieties of mint in cultivation, only some of which are good to eat. Those best known are spearmint and applemint. The best flavour comes from the youngest leaves at the top of the shoots and these can be used fresh or dried. Chopped mint is used to make sauces with meat and can be added to vegetables, pea soups, salads and yogurt dips.

Molasses

This is a by-product of sugar refining that is a rich source of vitamins B_1, B_2, B_6, pantothenic acid and biotin. It is also rich in iron, calcium, phosphorus and potassium. It can be used as a spread or in a similar way to honey in recipes.

Marjoram (Origanum spp.)

This tender perennial, often grown as an annual, provides fresh leaves for flavouring soups, stews, stuffings and other savoury dishes.

Mustard (Brassica nigro and Sinapsis alba)

Only the whole seed should be used, as powdered mustard commonly includes wheat flour. White seed has a milder flavour than dark seed. Whole mustard seed is used in pickling spice and with some meat and seafood dishes. The seed should be freshly crushed to make a variety of hot sauces.

Mung bean

See the entry under Beans.

Nasturtium (Tropaeolum majus)

This is the decorative hardy garden annual. Young leaves and flowers can be added to salads. Flower buds can be pickled in vinegar and used in the same way as capers. Seeds should be picked before they are ripe and pickled in vinegar to be used as capers, or they can be dried for later use in the same way as black pepper.

Nutmeg (Myristica fragrans)

Nutmeg is the seed of a tropical tree. It should be grated before use or purchased as a powder. Only a pinch should be used in any dish as it is poisonous in quantity. It can be used to flavour cakes, puddings, custards and fruit.

Olives (Olea europaea)

Olives are the fruit of the tree. Fresh olives have a very bitter taste. Whole olives are pickled when ripe or crushed to extract the oil. Olive oil can be used as a salad oil or for cooking. It is an easily digested, mono-unsaturated oil containing small amounts of vitamin E.

Onion (Allium cepa)

The onion is the edible bulb of the hardy biennial. There are also a number of hardy perennials where the bulb and leaves are used fresh for salads. Onion is best used fresh although dried onion is available.

Onion is included in many meat dishes, marinades, stocks, soups, and pickles as well as sauces and vegetable dishes. Shallots have a milder, more delicate flavour.

Palm Oil (Elaeis guineensis)

Palm oil and palm kernel oil are produced from the seed of this tropical palm. It is used in Nigeria as a general cooking oil and is a major component of some margarines.

Paprika (Capsicum annum)

Paprika is produced from the ripe large red fruit of this capsicum. Paprika can vary tremendously from a mild sweetness to close to the fiery taste of chilli where the seeds have been included. It should be purchased in small amounts, and used fresh to add colour and flavour to most savoury dishes, particularly beef stews.

Parsley (Carum petroselinum crispum)

This hardy biennial is rich in vitamins and minerals. It is used as a garnish for both hot and cold savoury dishes and as a flavouring for sauces and soups.

Parsnip (Patinaca sativa)

This very hardy root crop can be eaten boiled, fried or roasted and included in soups and stews.

Passion-fruit (Passiflora edulis)

The fruits of this perennial tropical climbing vine are best raw and is ripe when the purple skin becomes wrinkled.

Pawpaw, Papaya (Carica papaya)

The fruits of this tropical tree turn from green to yellow as they ripen. The flesh of the fruit is eaten raw. The fruit also makes an excellent marinade for meat.

Peas (Pisum sativum)

There are many strains of pea for use – fresh, frozen or dried. Peas are a useful component of many soups and stews and can be served as a vegetable. Young fresh peas should be simmered until just tender.

Dried pea flour is rich in protein and can be used to make thin pancakes or added to a flour mix for general baking. Peas also supply iron, zinc and B group vitamins. Try to keep intake of pulses below 1 oz per day. Split polished peas – dhal – are much more digestible.

Peach (Prunus persica)

These stoned fruit are available fresh or dried. They can be served fresh or cooked by baking or poaching. They supply some manganese to the diet.

Pears (Pyrus communis)

The fruit of this hardy tree stays very solid until ripe, when it can soften very quickly. Pears make an excellent addition to fruit stews.

Peanuts (Arachis hypogaea)

Peanuts are the seed of a tropical and subtropical annual. They have a high nutritional value, 30 per cent protein and 40–50 per cent oil. They contain high levels of vitamins B_1, B_2 and E as well as iron, calcium and phosphorus. Ground peanuts can be used as a substitute for part of the fat content in many recipes.

Peanut butter is produced by grinding the roasted nut after the germ has been removed.

Peanuts are known to cause mild discomfort and flatulence to some people when they are included in more than minimal amounts in the diet.

Pecan (Carya illinoensis)

The nuts of this large North American tree are eaten as a snack or used to flavour bread and cakes. With 37 per cent oil and 4.5 per cent protein they also contain calcium, potassium and iron with small amounts of B group vitamins and vitamin C.

Pepper – black (Piper nigrum)

Peppercorns are the whole fruit of a tropical climbing vine. They are best obtained whole and ground immediately before use.

Commercial pepper powder can occasionally be bulked out with wheat flour and should be avoided. Pepper should be added to most savoury dishes towards the end of cooking to give the best flavour. Whole peppercorns are used in pickling mixtures.

Peppermint (Mentha piperita)

The leaves can be added to desserts and sweets as a flavouring.

Persimmon, Date plum (Diospyros kaki)

The fruit of this warm temperate tree can be eaten fresh or cooked. They are yellow to red when ripe.

Pigeon Pea, Red Gram (Cajanus cajan)

This drought-resistant tropical legume is widely grown in India and the West Indies. These split peas may be cooked to form dhal or used in soups and stews. They contain 20 per cent protein and are a good source of iron, calcium, vitamins A, B_1 and B_2.

Pineapple (Annas comosus)

This tropical South American fruit has good vitamin A and C content. When fresh the fruit also contains an enzyme which digests protein and is excellent for marinading meat, but it should not be eaten by anyone with a recent history of digestive problems such as ulcers or recent food allergy, as this enzyme can attack the lining of the digestive system.

Canned pineapple is quite safe.

Pistachio (Pistacia vera)

The nuts of this small Mediterranean tree are eaten as snacks or used to decorate and flavour cakes and sweets. They contain 30 per cent oil and 22 per cent protein and are an excellent source of iron and potassium. Good quality nuts should appear pale green. They can also be used to make biscuits when ground into a flour.

Plums (Prunus spp.)

The fruit of this hardy tree freezes well and makes excellent jam – the stones should be removed before the sugar is added. Fresh or stewed plums can be eaten as a dessert or used as a filling for puddings and pies.

Poppy (Papaver somniferum)

This is the tiny hard seed of the opium poppy. They can be roasted gently before crushing, or covered with water, brought to the boil, then left to stand for three hours off the heat before crushing. They can be added to bread, cakes and pastries or used to flavour vegetables and sauces.

Potato (Solanum tuberosum)

The tuber of the potato is a good source of easily digested starch and the skin is rich in vitamins and minerals. In normal use the potato should be scrubbed clean and cooked by boiling or baking. The skin should be eaten for its full nutritional value. Any part of the potato that has been exposed to the light develops a green colour and should be discarded as it is poisonous.

Potato flour is produced from the starch of the potato and can be used in general baking, mixed with other flours.

Pumpkin seed

These nutritious seeds are very rich in iron. They contain 32 per cent protein and 55 per cent oil. They are also a good source of calcium and phosphorus. The seeds have a diuretic action.

Quinnoa (Chennopodium spp.)

This is another plant with its origins in the early civilisations of South America and is exported by Ecuador.

Quinnoa is 15 per cent protein. It has a slightly bitter flavour which can be removed from the grain by rinsing in boiling water. The whole grain can be cooked by boiling in water for 15 minutes and served like rice or it can be added to soups and stews.

For baking it should be ground into a flour just before use when it makes excellent biscuits and pancakes, although it imparts a slightly bitter flavour.

It is related to the weed 'fat hen' that grows easily in our gardens. Good crops of quinnoa can be grown from grain purchased in sealed packets from the health food shop. It threshes easily when ripe by rubbing the seed out of the husks.

Rape oil (Brassica napus)

A general cooking oil is obtained from the seed of this hardy annual.

Raspberries (Rubus idaeus)

This hardy cane fruit makes excellent jam. The fruit can be served fresh with shortbread and cream. The fruit is easily bruised and does not keep fresh long, but freezes well. It is an excellent source of vitamin C and a good source of iron.

Rhubarb (Rheum rhaponticum)

The fleshy leaf stalks of this herbaceous perennial are picked for eating in spring only. Mature stalks should not be eaten and the leaves are poisonous. The stem can be stewed with sugar or used to make jam. No water should be added.

Rice and Rice flour (Oryza sativa)

Rice is the seed of the cereal. Brown rice is mostly carbohydrate but contains 7.5 per cent protein, and small amounts of iron, calcium, and vitamins niacin and thiamin. Most rice is grown in standing water but 10 per cent of the world crop is grown on dry land. An outer bran layer covers the rice grain which can be removed together with the nutrients it contains to produce white rice. Vitamin B_1 is present in the bran but not in the white grain. Rice is commonly cooked simply by boiling. The liquid in which it is boiled should also be utilised in cooking as this also contains vitamins. In China this is often served as a drink. Glutinous rice is a variety that becomes sticky and sweet when cooked. It does not contain gluten.

Rice bran is a useful source of extra dietary fibre.

Rose Hips (Rosa canina, Rosa rugosa)

The fruit of the wild rose can be collected and used to make a vitamin-rich syrup. Dried rose-hips do not always contain vitamins.

Rosemary (Rosmarius officinalis)

The leaves of this small shrub are best used fresh to flavour poultry, meat and salads.

Rowan (Mountain Ash, Sorbus aucuparia)

The red berries of this small hardy tree make a vitamin-rich jelly to serve with meat and stews. They also make an excellent wine but it must be allowed to mature for several years or the flavour is harsh.

Safflower Oil (Carthamus tinctorius)

This is 78 per cent polyunsaturated oil, high in vitamin E. It is a good all-purpose cooking and salad oil.

Sage (Salvia officinalis)

The leaves of this small leafy shrub are best used fresh to flavour stuffings, soups and stews.

Sago (Metroxylon sagu)

Starch is extracted from the mature stem of this tropical palm tree. The flour is almost pure starch and can be used for general baking when mixed with other flours.

Savory – Summer (Satureia hortensis)

An annual Mediterranean herb used to flavour bread and sauces.

Savory – Winter (Satureia montana)

The leaves of this small hardy bush are used to flavour stews and other savoury dishes.

Sesame (Sesamum indicum)

Sesame seed comes from a tropical herbaceous annual. The seed can be ground into an oily paste called Tahini and it is also available as a nutty flavoured oil. Whole seed can be slightly roasted before use. The whole seed can be boiled as a main dish or mixed in bread and cakes. It is also used to make sweets, such as halva. Sesame oil can be used in savoury dishes and in salads.

Sesame contains 40 per cent fat and 18 per cent protein. It is very rich in potassium, calcium and iron, as well as the vitamin niacin.

Sesame oil is 44 per cent polyunsaturated and keeps well.

Sorghum and Sorghum flour (Sorghum vulgare)

Also known as great millet, kaffir corn, millo maize, American broom corn, Guinea corn. In India it is known as cholam or jowar, in Burma pyoung. Sorghum is widely grown in arid subtropical regions. The white grained Sorghum produces a grey flour which is excellent for all baking purposes and is the best general purpose gluten-free flour. It has good levels of protein, minerals and vitamins. Sorghum flour is easily digested and is mainly imported for the manufacture of baby foods.

Sorghum should not be used as a sprouting grain as the young shoots are very poisonous.

Soya (Glycine max)

Soya beans are grown in subtropical areas and harvested when ripe. Fresh bean pods can be eaten as a vegetable. Dried beans should be soaked overnight before boiling for at least two hours. They have an excellent nutritional value – 30–50 per cent protein, 15–30 per cent carbohydrate, 13–24 per cent oil. Black soya beans have the higher protein content, while yellow soya beans have the higher oil content. They are a good source of the minerals, calcium, iron, phosphorus, sodium and potassium and of the vitamins E, B_1, B_2 and B_5. Some people find soya beans indigestible and bitter.

Soy sauce is made by fermenting beans with flour. Often this is wheat flour and this sauce should not be used.

Soya bean curd, or tofu, is produced by soaking, grinding and then boiling the bean with water. The curd is precipitated from the resulting liquid and is much more palatable. Tofu can be used in bread, cakes, and pastry to improve texture and add to the nutritional value.

Squashes, Marrows and Pumpkins

See the entry under Marrows.

Strawberries (Fragaria spp.)

The fruits of this creeping perennial are a good source of vitamins. They are mostly eaten fresh or as jam. They can be frozen if they are later to be used in a cooked form, but do not freeze successfully to be eaten uncooked.

Sugar

Sugar is produced from the tropical sugar cane, Saccharum officinarum, and the temperate sugar beet, Beta vulgaris. The sugar produced from these crops is nutritionally identical and contains no vitamins or minerals.

Sunflower (Helianthus annuus)

The seeds of sunflower can be eaten raw or crushed and used in cakes and biscuits. Sunflower seeds have 22.5 per cent protein and are an excellent source of the minerals calcium, magnesium, iron and potassium as well as the vitamins thiamin, niacin, and E.

Sunflower oil is high in polyunsaturates and vitamin E and also contains vitamins A and D.

Sweet Corn (Corn on the cob, Zea mays)

Varieties of corn that have higher sugar levels in the grain are eaten as a vegetable. Sweet corn can be added to soups and stews. It is a good source of iron.

Sweet Potato (Ipomoea batatas)

This is the underground tuber of a subtropical or warm temperate climbing plant. The tuber is mostly starch but does include some protein and sugar. Sweet potatoes do not store well. They are normally cooked by boiling and mashing. The leaves can also be used as a vitamin-rich vegetable.

Tapioca, Cassava, Manioc (Manihot utilissima)

This is one of the most important food crops of the wet tropics. The swollen roots are often poisonous and partly for this reason tapioca is almost immune to attack by pests. The roots are peeled, crushed and the starch washed out of them. This starch is then dried to form pearl or flake and, more usefully, a fine flour. These have little nutritional value other than from the starch but the flour is useful for general baking when mixed with other flours.

Tarragon (Artemisia dracunculus)

This herb grows best in warm, dry conditions. Its leaves are best fresh in salads, sauces, pickles and with vinegar.

Tea (Camellia sinensis)

The dried, fermented leaves of this small tree contain caffeine and tannin. They are used both for hot and cold drinks and for flavouring stews and cakes.

Teff (Eragrostis abyssinica (Eragrostis tef))

This is a small-seeded relative of the millets. It is a staple crop of Ethiopia where it is made into a baked pancake called 'injera'.

Teff contains 14 per cent protein and 2 per cent fat. It is a good source of calcium, iron and thiamine, better than other cereal grains. It produces a brown flour with excellent baking qualities.

Only occasionally available in the UK.

Thyme (Thymus spp.)

The fresh leaves of this low-growing herb are best for flavouring stews, soups, stuffings and sauces.

Tofu

See also the entry under Soya. This is a curd made from processing soya beans. It is rich in protein, vitamins and minerals.

Tomato (Lycoparsicon esculentum)

The fruits of this tender perennial are a good source of vitamins A and C. They are eaten raw in salads or used to impart their flavour to many soups and savoury dishes.

Turnip and Swede (Brassic napa vars.)

These hardy biennial root crops can be used in soups and stews or mashed as a separate vegetable. The new leaves in spring can be eaten as spring greens.

Vanilla (Vanilla fragrans)

This flavouring comes from the long thin seed pod of a tropical climbing orchid. The pods can be kept in a jar of sugar when they import their flavour to the sugar, or the flavour can be extracted by steeping a pod in the liquid of the dish for one hour. Pods used in this way can be dried and used again. This pod can also be ground and used as a powder.

Walnut (Juglans regia)

The fruit of a large hardy tree. They contain 12 per cent protein and high levels of potassium, calcium, magnesium, iron and zinc. Young green fruits can be pickled in vinegar. Walnut oil is extracted from ripe nuts and is high in polyunsaturates. Walnuts can be used in both sweet and savoury dishes.

Water Chestnut, Caltrops (Trapa natans)

The large seed of this water plant can be eaten raw, boiled or roasted.

Wild Rice (Zizania aquatica)

This is an aquatic grass native to North America. Its seeds can be eaten boiled or steamed. It has a high protein and vitamin content.

Yam (Dioscorea spp.)

These are the underground tubers of tropical climbing plants. They form a staple food crop in parts of Africa but contribute little other than starch to the diet. They store well in ventilated racks.

Brown yam flour has some good baking qualities and a mild flavour. It can be used for general baking on its own or mixed with other flours.

Dairy products

Most dairy products are produced from the milk of cows, sheep, goats and occasionally from yaks, buffalo, camels and horses.

Milk

Cows' milk is an important source of calcium and riboflavin with smaller quantities of other vitamins and minerals. It contains close to 4 per cent fat.

Low-fat milks have lower levels of fat and vitamins A and D but the same amount of calcium. Low-fat milk should not be given to young children. Give them full fat milk.

Most people of European origin are able to digest milk easily but some people produce little or none of the enzyme lactase that digests the sugar in milk. The undigested sugar feeds bacteria which cause discomfort in the abdomen. If this is the case the quantity of milk in the diet should be restricted. Most children are able to digest milk without difficulty.

Fresh milk and long-life milk once opened should be kept under refrigeration for no more than two days.

Fresh milk or dried milk can be used in baking to improve the taste and texture of a wide range of breads, cakes, pancakes, biscuits, soups and stews.

Cream

Single cream is 21 per cent fat, whipping cream is 21 per cent fat and double cream is 48 per cent fat. Cream is a good source of vitamin A with smaller quantities of vitamins E and D. Cream is a major component of many sweets and is used as a filling or topping for many other sweet dishes. It should be stored under refrigeration and any dishes using it should also be stored under refrigeration for a maximum of two days.

Eggs

These are an excellent source of most vitamins and minerals. Some people may wish to avoid recipes that include eggs which are not subsequently cooked.

Cheese

Cheese is an excellent source of calcium, protein and riboflavin and a good source of most minerals and many other vitamins. It may contain up to 35 per cent fat.

The hardest cheeses, such as Parmesan, can be stored in a cool place for several years. These are usually grated as a topping on savoury dishes.

Semi-hard cheeses, like Cheddar, are best kept refrigerated but can be kept in a cool place if allowed to dry out. They make excellent cheeses for savoury cheese dishes.

Softer cheeses, like Edam, need to be refrigerated. They tend to go very stringy when cooked.

Soft cheeses, like Camembert, become very soft when ripe and cannot be stored beyond this point.

Cottage cheese contains only 4 per cent fat and must be kept refrigerated and eaten quickly. It can be served with salad or hot as a filling for rolls or pancakes.

Cheese does not give rise to the same digestive disorders as milk as it contains no lactose.

Roquefort cheese contains breadcrumbs and should be avoided.

Yogurt

Always buy natural yogurt and add your own flavourings, as sometimes wheat flour is added as a filler to flavoured yogurt.

Yogurt will keep longer than milk and contains lower lactose levels than milk. It is an excellent source of calcium, protein and riboflavin. Like milk it also provides many other nutrients. Yogurt can be eaten on its own, with fruit or jam, or added to bread, cakes, soups and stews, or used to thicken sauces. It should not be boiled.

Fromage Frais

This is a low-fat soft cheese made from skimmed milk. It is a good source of calcium and can be used in place of cream in many recipes.

Butter

This is the almost pure fat component of milk. It gives an excellent flavour to any baking in which it is included. Butter is an excellent source of vitamin E.

Meat

Meat provides the full range of amino acids needed to build protein and is the main source of iron and zinc. It also contains a full range of other minerals. There is little variation in the nutritional value between the different types of meat. The nutritional value is present in the meat fibre not in the fat, which is a good source of energy only. Uncooked meat can be kept refrigerated for several days but should be kept separate from cooked foods. If both are kept in the same domestic refrigerator then the raw meat should be kept on the bottom shelves, below any cooked food.

Beef, Mutton, Lamb, Pork

These meats can have a relatively high fat content. Visible fat can be removed before cooking to reduce the fat level that is eaten. Different cuts of meat are priced according to tenderness and fat content.

Veal

Calf meat has a lower fat content than the meat from adult cattle.

Chicken, Goose, Duck

Fat is usually present in a layer beneath the skin and in the body cavity. Goose and duck must be well cooked to ensure that all this fat has melted. Skinned meat fillets have a low fat content but are not suitable for roasting or dry cooking methods. Frozen birds must be completely thawed before cooking and the cavity should not be stuffed. Flesh should be plump and firm when raw.

Rabbit, Hare, Turkey, Venison

Very low fat levels within the meat meant that roasting can produce a very dry meat. Cover with foil to hold the moisture within the flesh, or baste with added fat or use moist cooking methods.

Liver

Liver is the best source of iron in the diet and also has high levels of vitamins A, riboflavin, niacin, B_6, pantothenic acid, biotin, folacin, B_{12}, C and D. It should be cooked as little as possible.

Kidney

This is also a very good source of iron and vitamins thiamin, riboflavin, nicotinic acid, B_6, B_{12}, C and E. It should be cooked as little as possible.

Fish and other seafood

Fresh fish should be bright in colour and the eyes should be full and clear, not dull and sunken. Gills should be red and the flesh should feel firm. Fresh fish should be kept in ice at 0°C/32°F. The temperature of a domestic refrigerator is too warm for keeping fish. Oily fish in particular will start to spoil within 48 hours at 4°C. Fish should be gutted as soon as possible after purchase.

All fish are a good source of minerals in the diet.

Sole, Plaice, Dab and Flounder

These small flat-fish have little fat but are a good source of proteins and minerals. They can be cooked whole and served as individual portions, or filleted. Cook by steaming, grilling, baking or frying.

Brill, Halibut, Turbot

These large flat-fish are a good source of proteins and minerals and contain little fat. They are usually cut into thick steaks and cooked using a moist method.

Cod, Coley, Haddock, Hake, Pollack, Whiting

These members of the cod family are a good source of proteins and minerals and contain little fat. Their mild flavoured white flesh is best poached or steamed. Cod liver is an excellent source of vitamins A, D and E.

Salmon and Trout

Both of these are now available as farmed fish, which has brought the price down. A good source of proteins and minerals with up to 10 per cent fat. The mild flavoured flesh of trout is best poached or steamed. The stronger flavour of salmon can complement a wider variety of cooking methods and sauces.

Herring, Mackerel, Sardine

These fish can contain up to 13 per cent oil. They are also excellent as a source of vitamins D and E. They must be eaten very fresh. They can be fried or grilled or pickled in vinegar.

Tuna, Swordfish

A good source of proteins and minerals with 5 per cent fat.

These fish have a very firm meat that can be grilled or barbecued. They can also be braised. The meat becomes tough if overcooked.

CARTILAGINOUS FISH – NO HARD BONES

These are all good sources of vitamin E.

Ray and Skate

A good source of proteins and minerals with little fat. The wings contain a layer of flesh on each side of an inedible cartilaginous web. They are best cooked by moist methods.

Dogfish

Solid white meat without bones that can be cooked by steaming, grilling, baking or frying. The skin is not eaten.

Shark

A good source of proteins and minerals with 5 per cent fat.

The larger sharks have a very solid, boneless flesh, that can be grilled or stewed in a similar way to pork. The skin is not eaten.

CRUSTACEANS

These are all good sources of many minerals, especially iodine.

Lobster, Crab

These must be eaten very fresh. For this reason they should be obtained alive when they should move actively. They are killed by being dropped into boiling water. The head sac and the intestine needs to be removed and discarded. The gills are discarded after cooking. Lobster and crab are best cooked by boiling or steaming as they tend to dry out rather easily.

Prawns and Shrimps

These must be cooked fresh, within a few hours of being caught, as they deteriorate rapidly. The heads and the shell are removed before eating. The shells can be eaten and can be a useful source of calcium.

MOLLUSCS

Bivalve Molluscs, Oysters

These should be alive when cooked, or eaten raw. The shell should be tight shut. A short, stout knife is inserted between the shells close to the hinge, where a sharp twist will break the shells apart. The muscle is then cut where it joins the upper and the lower shell.

They can be grilled, deep-fried or simmered in soups and stews.

Mussels

These should be alive and the shell tight shut. The shell is scrubbed clean and the beard removed before the shell is forced open, or the mussels are boiled vigorously for five minutes after which any mussels that remain closed are discarded. Mussels can be steamed, grilled, baked or used in soups and stews.

Other ingredients

Raising Agents

Baking powder should not be used. This often contains wheat flour as a filler. There is no need to mix a gluten-free baking powder beforehand, simply use the pure raising agents as required.

BICARBONATE OF SODA, SODIUM BICARBONATE
This white powder releases carbon dioxide when it is mixed with an acid solution and warmed. These gas bubbles expand causing the mixture to rise. If there is no acidity in the mixture, bicarbonate of soda and cream of tartar should be added in equal quantities and mixed in well.

CREAM OF TARTAR
This is a weak acid in powder form for activating bicarbonate of soda.

TARTARIC ACID
This is another weak acid that can be used with bicarbonate of soda as a raising agent.

Citric Acid

This is available in powder form and can be used as a substitute for the acidity of lemon juice in recipes. It is particularly useful for winemaking.

Salt, Sodium Chloride

Western diets often contain too much salt. The recipes suggest salt to taste, but keep the quantity as low as possible. Iodised table salt can be an important source of iodine.

ALL MANUFACTURED FOODS

The Coeliac Society produces a food list each year of manufactured foods that do not contain gluten.

You cannot always tell by looking at the contents label on the food packet.

Wheat flour may be used to help the food pass through machinery, to stop food sticking to baking trays or as a bulking agent to help distribute spices within a mixture.

This wheat flour is not declared on the contents label.

Food lists produced by supermarkets, chemists shops and health food stores often contain errors.

You are strongly advised to purchase a copy of the food list from the Coeliac Society and to keep it up to date. The address can be found on page xiv.

Forbidden: food ingredients to avoid

Wheat: grain containing high levels of gluten.
Bulgar: soaked and dried wheat.
Durum: a type of wheat.
Strong flour, bread flour, brown flour, wholemeal flour, granary flour: all made from wheat.

Oats: contain some protein similar to wheat gluten but may not cause problems for all coeliacs. Best avoided.
Barley: contains some protein similar to wheat gluten.
Rye: contains some protein similar to wheat gluten.
Triticale: contains some protein similar to wheat gluten.
Spelt: contains some protein similar to wheat gluten.
Semolina: made from wheat.
Couscous. made from wheat.
Pasta, macaroni, spaghetti: made from wheat.

Baking powder: may contain wheat flour.

Stock cubes: may contain wheat flour.

Mustard powder: may contain wheat flour.

Soy sauce: this is normally soya beans fermented with wheat flour. Check the food list for brands that do not contain wheat flour.

Suet in packets: may contain wheat flour to stop the suet sticking together.

Equipment

Beware of contamination by wheat flour if the same equipment is being used to prepare both gluten-free and non-gluten-free meals.

Food Mixers

If you are cooking on a regular basis, a bowl-type mixer is indispensable. A spare bowl can be very useful.

Food Processors

Many of the bread and cake recipes are improved by the addition of puréed banana, sweet chestnut, tofu, apple or carrot. It is almost impossible to blend these to a smooth texture by hand. Choose a processor that is easy to take apart and clean and can cope with quantities of food.

Grain Mill

This attachment is available for the Kenwood mixer only. I find it indispensable. Using a grain mill to grind the whole seed removes the possibility of contamination that arises in a commercial mill where the same equipment may be used to grind wheat flours and gluten-free flours.

The grain mill will grind most hard dry seeds to a flour. It can be used to grind amaranth, beans, millet, lentils, mustard, peas, quinnoa, sorghum, teff and most spices.

Oily seeds, such as sesame and nuts, can be put through the grain mill but tend to clog the grinding mechanism. Rice does not grind well in this attachment. Pearl sago and tapioca are too hard to grind into flour.

Pressure Cooker

This is very useful to reduce the cooking times for soups and stews, particularly for those containing pulses, which can take a long time to cook.

Cooking Paper

Beware, some brands of 'rice paper' are made using wheat flour.

Use silicone-coated non-stick baking parchment to prevent baking from sticking to tins. Greaseproof paper or aluminium foil are not nearly as effective.

SECTION 2: RECIPES

Gluten-free flour mixes

Most gluten-free, wheat-free flours bake much better in a mixture than on their own. Gluten-free flour mixes are now available in many supermarkets, or from specialist GF suppliers. Some people who need a gluten-free diet cannot tolerate Soya, and others find buckwheat has too strong a flavour or is indigestible. Pea flours or gram flours can also be indigestible in large quantities. Coarsely ground flours such as ground rice and polenta can be used in bread, or heavy fruit cakes or parkin, but much finer flours are needed for light cakes and biscuits.

If you only make occasional use of your flour mixtures, keep your mix in a sealed container in the deep freeze.

General purpose flour mix 1
Take an equal measure from each of the gluten-free flours that you have been able to obtain and mix together. Use this mixture for all recipes!

General purpose flour mix 2
6 oz or 175 g rice flour
4 oz or 100 g maize flour or dry polenta
6 oz or 175 g sorghum flour

Savoury flour mix 1
6 oz or 175 g rice flour
6 oz or 175 g maize flour or dry polenta
2 oz or 50 g pea flour or gram flour
2 oz or 50 g Soya flour

Savoury flour mix 2
6 oz or 175 g rice flour
6 oz or 175 g maize flour or dry polenta
4 oz or 100 g buckwheat flour

Self-raising flour mix
Add 1 teaspoon of bicarbonate of soda and 1 teaspoon of cream of tartar to 1 lb or 450 g of flour mix and mix together well.

Sweet flour mix 1
6 oz or 175 g rice flour
6 oz or 175 g cornflour
4 oz or 100 g fine potato flour

Sweet flour mix 2
8 oz or 250 g rice flour
8 oz or 250 g sweet chestnut flour

Sweet flour mix 3
8 oz or 250 g rice flour
8 oz or 250 g ground almonds

Recipes for feeding children

It is recommended that no child under six months be given any food containing gluten.

It is important that an older child is *not* put on a gluten-free diet before the diagnosis of the coeliac condition has been confirmed by a doctor. The change in diet may make diagnosis more difficult.

Recipes for the Coeliac Child

After the coeliac condition or wheat intolerance has been diagnosed you must ensure that *all* food eaten by the child is gluten-free.

The amount of fat and refined sugar should be restricted in the first month after diagnosis of the coeliac condition, as the lining of the intestines has to regrow in the absence of gluten before these can be fully absorbed.

Once a child with the coeliac condition is on a totally gluten-free diet, they should be completely normal and healthy.

Six months to twelve months

Salt and salty foods, as well as heavily spiced foods, should be avoided and the amount of sugar and fat should be kept to the minimum. Salt and sugar should not be added to foods.

The food should be presented in the form of a purée at first, served lukewarm or cold, but always freshly prepared. When you see your baby starting to chew, small soft lumps of food can be included, but do not allow your baby to have hard, lumpy foods like peanuts, which might cause choking.

Do not give a baby too many different flavours at once, and give any purée after the milk feed.

Suitable first foods for a six-month-old baby

Mashed ripe banana, avocado, apple, pear.

Cooked egg yolk, purée of cottage cheese, purée of chicken, purée of boiled or steamed fish. Yogurt without lumps.

Purée of carrots, leeks, potatoes, cauliflower, lentils, parsnips, brown rice, or any combination. In each case the vegetables should be steamed or boiled without salt until soft, and then well mashed. A little formula milk can also be added to the purée.

Do not give a coeliac baby rusks to chew, give sticks of carrot or apple.

Pancakes are very useful when a child is ready to move on to more solid food.

Sorghum flour is easily digested and it is mainly imported for the manufacture of baby foods.

ONE YEAR ONWARDS

As soon as a child can cope with a range of food flavours and texture, often before one year, you can use the wide range of recipes in this book. Still keep down the proportion of salt, sugar and fat in the diet but don't eliminate them.

A child needs a wide variety of foods for healthy growth. Don't restrict yourself to cooking a few of the easiest recipes, and use as wide a range of gluten-free ingredients as possible.

It is important that a child with the coeliac condition is not made to feel different from other children. It will help the child if all your family eat gluten-free meals including gluten-free cake and biscuits and, if you can, prepare gluten-free sausages and beefburgers so that they feel they are eating the same types of food as other children.

Birthday cakes

Sponge Layer Cake

- Make an 8 inch/20 cm vanilla sponge cake and an 8 inch/20 cm chocolate sponge cake. See page 123.
- Sandwich the two cakes together with a layer of chocolate butter-cream icing. See page 133.
- Extra layers can be added for more variety.
- Spread the top of the cake with white icing or butter-cream icing.

Marble Cake

- Prepare the basic sponge mixture and divide this into three portions.
- Flavour and colour each portion of the mixture separately and differently.
- Pour each portion into the same sponge tin and stir very briefly – twice round with the handle of a wooden spoon is enough.
- Cook and ice in the usual way.

Variations
- Layer cakes can also be made using Almond Sponge Cake or Bataclan. See pages 125 and 126.
- Many children like a good fruit cake for a birthday cake: try the Dundee Cake. See page 127.

Children's party ideas

Prepare all gluten-free fare for your own children's parties.

Cheese selection		Baked banana	
Sausage rolls	page 91	Jelly	
Sausages on sticks (not for the youngest children)	page 89	Trifles	page 161
Beefburgers	page 76	Sponge cakes in individual paper cases	
Baked potatoes		Chocolate fondue	page 139
Small chicken joints		Biscuits	page 140
Potato crisps – check food list		Gingerbread men	page 142
		Marsh mallow	page 198
Fresh fruit		Ice-cream – check food list	
Dried fruit salad			

Filled Sandwiches

- Use carrot bread for savoury fillings and banana bread for sweet fillings.
- Cook the bread in individual pattie tins.
- Split in two and spread with soft butter.

Savoury fillings	Sweet fillings
Cheese	Honey
Sardines in oil or brine	Jam
Tuna in oil or brine	Molasses/black treacle
Green salad	Maple syrup
Bean sprouts	Banana
Cold meat	Fresh fruit slices

Check the food list for all manufactured sauces and dressings.

Breakfasts

Bacon and Egg Pizza

A substantial breakfast

MAKES 4 PORTIONS

For the base
4 oz or 100 g grated carrot
1 egg
¼ pint or 150 ml milk or water
8 oz or 225 g gluten-free flour mix
1 tablespoon olive oil
pinch salt

½ teaspoon bicarbonate of soda
¼ teaspoon cream of tartar
1 teaspoon sugar

For the topping
2 eggs
4 rashers bacon

- Beat the carrot to a smooth purée with the milk and egg. This is best done in a liquidiser.
- Mix all the dry ingredients for the base together with one tablespoon oil.
- Fold the flour mixture into the purée. Do not overmix and do not leave to stand at this point or you will lose the light structure to the bread dough.
- Spread the dough out to fit a 10 inch/25 cm square baking tray.
- Cover with the rashers of bacon.
- Bake in a preheated oven, gas mark 7, 425°F, 220°C, for 20 minutes.
- Pour the eggs on top of the pizza after 15 minutes cooking and return to the oven until cooked.

Variations:
Use 1 large banana or 4 oz/100 g grated apple or tofu in place of the carrot.

Kedgeree

A traditional English breakfast or lunch dish.

MAKES 2 TO 3 PORTIONS

8 oz or 225 g cold cooked fish
   include some smoked fish for
   extra flavour
2 oz or 50 g rice

1 hard-boiled egg
1 oz or 25 g butter
salt to taste
fresh ground black pepper to taste

- Boil the rice until cooked and drain.
- Divide the fish into small flakes.
- Slice the boiled egg thinly.
- Melt the butter in a large pan and stir in all the ingredients.
- Continue stirring until hot and ready to serve.

Rice and Ham

A hot breakfast or lunch dish.

MAKES 2 TO 3 PORTIONS

8 oz or 225 g cold, cooked,
   diced ham
2 oz or 50 g rice
2 oz or 50 g cooked sweet corn

2 oz or 50 g cooked green peas
1 oz or 25 g butter
salt to taste
fresh ground black pepper to taste

- Boil the rice until cooked and then drain it.
- Melt the butter in a large pan and stir in all the ingredients.
- Continue stirring until hot and ready to serve.

Rissoles

MAKES 4

4 oz or 100 g cooked mashed
  potato
1 oz or 25 g finely chopped
  cooked onion
2 oz or 50 g pea flour or
  gram flour

1 egg
salt to taste
4 oz or 100 g cooked minced beef

- Beat the egg, flour, potato and onion together and then stir in the cooked minced beef.
- Fry spoonfuls of the mixture until golden brown on each side.

Variations
- Use sorghum flour in place of pea flour.

Fish Cakes

PER PERSON

3 oz or 75 g cold mashed potatoes
3 oz or 75 g cold, cooked white
  fish fillet
½ oz or 12 g butter
1 teaspoon chopped fresh parsley

¼ teaspoon pepper and salt to
  taste
¼ teaspoon lemon juice to taste
1 egg
1 oz or 25 g potato flour

- Beat together the potato, fish, butter, parsley, lemon juice and seasoning.
- Divide the mixture into two portions and shape on a surface dusted with potato flour.
- Dip each portion in egg to coat the cake all over.
- Fry in hot oil in a large frying pan over a medium heat.
- Turn when golden brown.
- Serve when both sides are golden brown.

Polenta

An Italian breakfast dish that I was first served while on holiday in Austria.

PER PERSON

2 oz or 50 g maize corn meal or   salt to taste
  polenta
¼ pint or 150 ml water or milk

- Mix the corn meal and water together with the salt and bring to the boil slowly in a heavy bottomed pan.
- Simmer gently, stirring frequently for 30 minutes until a thick porridge is formed.
- Add more milk if the porridge is too thick.
- Serve with cream or milk, or with honey or syrup.

Variations
- A richer polenta can be made by adding ½ oz/12 g butter to the corn meal before cooking.
- Cooked polenta can be allowed to go cold before cutting into squares. These can then be fried or covered with grated cheese and then grilled.

Quinnoa Porridge

A very quick to make, easily digested breakfast.

PER PERSON

2 oz or 50 g quinnoa grain   ¼ pint or 150 ml water

- Place the grain in a fine sieve and pour a kettle of boiling water through to wash the grain well.
- Simmer the grain in ¼ pint or 150 ml water for 15 minutes and then drain.
- Serve with cream.

Kasha

This is a traditional Eastern European breakfast with a strong flavour.

MAKES 4 PORTIONS

8 oz or 225 g buckwheat
½ oz or 12 g butter

salt to taste
water

- Roast the buckwheat in a dry frying pan until the grains are a light golden colour.
- Put the grain in an ovenproof dish and add enough boiling water to cover the grain.
- Add the butter and salt.
- Bake in a preheated oven, gas mark 2, 300°F, 150°C, for three hours.
- Serve with milk, maple syrup or honey.

Teff Porridge

A nutritious Ethiopian staple meal.

PER PERSON

2 oz or 50 g teff flour
Water or milk as required

salt to taste

- Using a thick bottomed saucepan, stir the dry teff flour in the pan over the heat until it starts to smell as though it was roasting.
- Stir in water or milk gradually until the porridge is boiling with the desired consistency.
- Turn down the heat and leave to simmer gently for five minutes.
- Serve with milk, maple syrup or honey.

Muesli

This muesli is an excellent source of dietary fibre.

SERVES 4

Equal quantities of:
sunflower seeds
chopped dates
chopped figs
sultanas

banana chips
chopped mixed nuts
pine nuts
cooked flake rice
honey

- Mix 2 oz/50 g of each ingredient and keep the mixture in a sealed container in a cool dry place for up to a week.
- Serve with milk or pour on a fruit juice.

Variations
- Add equal quantities of any of the following:
  cooked flake millet
  shredded coconut

Other breakfasts

Cornflakes – try serving
  breakfast cornflakes or puff
  rice with stewed fruit
Puff rice
Bacon and eggs
Boiled egg
Scrambled eggs

Baked beans – check you use a
  gluten-free brand
Pancakes – see pancake recipes
Herring/Cod's roe, fried
Kippers
Grilled herring

Lunch and snack dishes

Cheese Omelette

MAKES 2 SMALL OR 1 LARGE PORTION

2 eggs
2 oz or 50 g Gouda cheese
1 oz or 25 g butter or olive oil

finely chopped chives
salt and fresh ground black
pepper to taste

- Beat the eggs and stir in the chives, salt and pepper.
- Cut the cheese into very thin slices or use grated cheese.
- Heat the grill.
- Heat the butter or olive oil in a frying pan and pour in eggs when it is hot.
- Immediately place the cheese over the omelette.
- As soon as the bottom of the omelette is almost cooked place the frying pan under the grill until the cheese melts (Don't put the handle under the grill!)
- Flip the sides of the omelette to the centre and serve immediately.

Variations
- Any of the following can be added to the omelette before cooking:
    - 1 tomato, sliced thinly
    - 1 oz or 25 g mushrooms
- A lighter omelette can be made by separating the egg yolk and white and beating them separately before folding them together.

Herb Omelette

MAKES 1 LARGE OR 2 SMALL PORTIONS

2 eggs   salt to taste
½ oz or 12 g chopped fresh chives   1 oz or 25 g butter
½ oz or 12 g chopped fresh parsley   1 oz or 25 g grated cheese
¼ oz or 6 g chopped fresh marjoram

- Beat the eggs and stir in the herbs and salt.
- Heat the butter in a frying pan, pour in the omelette and sprinkle the cheese on top.
- Cook until the omelette has set and the cheese on top has started to melt.
- Roll the omelette before serving and always serve it freshly cooked.
- Cook a separate omelette for each person.

Italian Omelette

MAKES 2 PORTIONS

2 eggs   2 chopped olives
½ oz or 12 g chopped fresh chives   1 oz or 25 g grated cheese
½ oz or 12 g chopped fresh parsley   salt to taste
4 oz or 100 g cooked potato   olive oil
1 tomato

- Beat the eggs and stir in the herbs, potato, tomato, olives and salt.
- Heat the oil in a frying pan, pour in the omelette and sprinkle the cheese on top.
- Cook slowly until the omelette is set and golden brown.
- Lift the omelette and add a little more oil before flipping to cook the other side.

Pizza in a Pan

SERVES 3 TO 4

For the base
4 oz or 100 g grated carrot
1 egg
¼ pint or 150 ml milk or water
8 oz or 225 g gluten-free flour mix
salt to taste
½ teaspoon bicarbonate of soda
¼ teaspoon cream of tartar
2 tablespoons olive oil
2 oz or 50 g grated cheese

For the topping, use any or all of the following:
2 oz or 50 g tomato purée
2 oz or 50 g chopped tomato
4 oz or 100 g grated cheese
1 oz or 25 g chopped olives
2 oz or 50 g anchovy fillets
1 teaspoon dried mixed herbs
2 tablespoons olive oil

- Beat the carrot to a smooth purée with the milk and egg. This is best done in a liquidiser.
- Mix all the dry ingredients for the base together with two tablespoons oil.
- Fold the flour mixture into the purée. Do not overmix and do not leave to stand or you will lose the light structure to the pizza dough.
- Spread the batter to fit a 10 inch/25 cm frying pan.
- Place the pan over a low heat. Use one tablespoon olive oil to cook each side of the pizza base for about five to ten minutes until brown.
- While cooking the second side, spread the top with tomato purée and scatter the chopped tomato, grated cheese, herbs and olives all over.
- Place the anchovies on top and sprinkle with a tablespoon olive oil.
- When the underside is cooked place the pizza under a preheated grill for 3 minutes. (Transfer to a grill pan if your frying pan has a plastic handle.)
- Serve when the cheese has melted.

Variations
- Use 1 large banana or 4 oz/100 g tofu in place of the carrot.
- Use a base of mashed potato.
- Use a base of grated raw potato tossed in corn oil.

Quiche Lorraine

Serves 4

For the base
8 oz prepared shortcrust pastry.
  See page 166 for ingredients.

For the filling
4 oz or 100 g diced bacon
1 small onion, coarsely chopped
For the custard
2 eggs

2 egg yolks
5 fl oz or 175 ml milk
2 fl oz or 60 ml double cream
2 oz or 50 g grated cheese or
  cream cheese
salt to taste
fresh ground black pepper
  to taste
grated nutmeg.

- **To prepare the base**, roll out the pastry to line a 7½ inch/19 cm flan tin.
- Cook the empty pastry shell in a preheated oven, gas mark 7, 425°F, 220°C, for 12 to 15 minutes or until light brown.
- Brush the pastry with a little beaten egg and return to the oven for 5 minutes.
- Fry the bacon and onion in butter until lightly browned all over and place in the baked pastry.
- **To prepare the custard**, beat the eggs and yolks, beat in the milk and cream and then the cheese and seasoning.
- Pour this beaten mixture over the bacon and onion.
- Sprinkle nutmeg on top.
- Bake in a preheated oven, gas mark 5, 375°F, 190°C, for 25–30 minutes, or until firm and golden brown.
- Serve hot or cold.

Other Quiches

Prepare the pastry case and the custard in the same way as for quiche lorraine. Vary the filling to provide variety.

SPINACH AND CREAM CHEESE
- For the filling clean 2 lb/900 g fresh spinach leaves and cook with 1 oz/25 g butter in a heavy saucepan for 8 minutes. Stir from time to time.

- Use cream cheese in place of double cream in preparing the custard.

LEEK AND CELERY
- For the filling clean 2 medium leeks and 1 stick of celery.
- Slice these into thin rings and cook with 1 oz/25 g butter in a heavy saucepan for 8 minutes. Stir from time to time.

MUSHROOM AND TOMATO
- For the filling slice 6 oz/175 g fresh tomato and 6 oz/175 g fresh button mushrooms and place in the pastry case.

FLAKED FISH
- For the filling use 6 oz/175 g any cooked and flaked fish. Tinned tuna and tinned salmon both make an excellent quiche.

Potato Crust Quiche

SERVES 4

1 lb or 450 g potatoes
2 oz or 50 g butter
1 oz or 25 g cornflour
1 oz or 25 g rice flour
7 oz or 200 g tinned salmon or
tuna in brine
2 eggs

4 fl oz or 125 ml cream, yoghurt
or milk
2 oz or 50 g grated Cheddar
cheese
salt and pepper to taste
parsley to garnish

- Boil the potatoes until soft, then drain and mash them with the butter and flour.
- Spread the potato mixture evenly over the base of the flan dish.
- Drain the tinned fish and spread evenly over the top.
- Beat the eggs and cream, yoghurt or milk together and season before pouring over the fish.
- Sprinkle the cheese over the top.
- Cook at gas mark 5, 375°F, 190°C for 25–30 minutes, or until lightly set and golden.
- Garnish with parsley and serve hot or cold.

Cheese Pudding

SERVES 2

2 eggs
4 oz or 100 g grated cheese
1 oz or 25 g savoury gluten-
   free flour mix
¼ pint or 150 ml milk

1 oz or 25 g fresh ground
   mustard seed
salt to taste
fresh ground black pepper to taste
1 tomato

- Beat the eggs and then beat in the remaining ingredients.
- Place the mixture in a greased baking dish.
- Slice the tomato and place on the top of the mixture.
- Bake in a preheated oven, gas mark 6, 400°F, 200°C, for 20 minutes.

Variations
- Add 4 oz or 100 g cooked, diced potato and stir into the mixture.

Liver and Bacon

SERVES 4

1 medium onion
1 lb or 450 g liver
4 oz or 100 g bacon
14 oz or 400 g tinned tomatoes
4 fl oz or 125 ml pure orange
   juice

pinch dried mixed herbs
salt to taste
fresh ground black pepper to
   taste.

- Chop the onions finely and fry in a little oil until translucent.
- Cut the bacon into 2 inch pieces and add to the pan.
- Cut the liver into ½ inch strips and add to the pan.
- Fry for 4 minutes over a moderate heat, turning the liver and bacon constantly.
- Add the tinned tomatoes, orange juice and dried mixed herbs.
- Simmer carefully for 10 minutes before serving.
- Take care not to overcook the liver.

Cottage Pie

SERVES 4

1 medium onion	14 oz or 400 g tinned tomatoes
4 medium potatoes	2 cloves garlic, crushed
4 medium carrots	salt to taste
1 small swede	fresh ground black pepper to taste
1 lb or 450 g minced beef	1 tomato to garnish

- Cook and mash the boiled potato.
- Cook and mash the swede and carrot together.
- Chop the onion and fry in a little oil until translucent.
- Add the minced beef to the frying pan and cook for 8 minutes over a moderate heat. Stir while cooking.
- Add the tinned tomatoes and crushed garlic to the minced beef and bring to a simmer.
- Transfer the minced beef and tomato to a casserole.
- Layer the mashed swede and carrot above the minced beef.
- Layer the mashed potato above the carrot.
- Pattern the potato with the back of a fork.
- Add a sliced tomato to decorate the top before baking.
- Bake in a preheated oven, gas mark 6, 400°F, 200°C for 20 minutes.

Cauliflower Cheese

SERVES 4

1 medium cauliflower

For the sauce

1 oz or 25 g cornflour	salt and pepper to taste
½ pint or 280 ml milk, meat juice or stock	4 oz or 100 g grated cheese

- Take one medium cauliflower or solid white broccoli. Remove any old and damaged leaves, but any young leaves should be kept.
- Turn the cauliflower upside down and split the stem from the base to separate the head into portions.

- Place in a pan with the head upwards and cover with water. Boil for 15–20 minutes until the stem is tender.
- Mix the cornflour into a paste with a little *cold* milk or water.
- Stir in the remaining milk, meat juice or stock without heating and add the grated cheese.
- Now slowly heat the sauce to simmer, stirring continuously.
- Simmer very gently for 5 minutes.
- Pour the sauce over the cooked cauliflower and brown slightly under the grill before serving.

Variations
- Many other vegetables can be served in white sauce as a lunch dish. Try carrot and peas, leek and potato, beetroot.

Tuna and Rice

Tuna is a very solid fish. One small tin may serve several people but the quantity per person can be varied to suit personal preferences.

PER PERSON

2 oz or 50 g long grain rice   *tuna fish*

- Cover the rice with ½ pint water for each 2 oz/50 g portion.
- White rice should be boiled for 20 minutes until soft but not disintegrating. Brown rice should be boiled for 40 minutes. Then drain the rice. The water in which the rice has been boiled can be used to make sauces or soups.
- For a fluffy texture, rinse the hot cooked rice well with boiling water.
- Flake the tuna, mix with the hot cooked rice and serve immediately.

- Serve with a gluten-free mayonnaise or a white sauce.

Variations
- Many other cooked fish can be flaked and served in this way as a lunch dish.
- Try adding cooked peas or cooked sweet corn to the dish.
- Serve with **Mushroom and Onion Sauce**.

olive oil	*4 oz or 100 g mushrooms*
1 medium onion	*herbs as available (thyme, sage, rosemary etc)*

- Chop the onion and drop into the oil, frying gently till beginning to turn transparent.
- Chop the mushroom and add to the onion.
- Fry together until the onion is golden brown and the mushroom softened.
- Now add a tablespoon of boiling water and simmer for five minutes.

Corned Beef and Hash Browns – Canadian Style

PER PERSON	
2 oz or 50 g gluten-free corned beef	*1 egg, beaten (this will coat many slices of corned beef)*
4 oz or 100 g raw potato	

- Peel and grate the raw potato. A food processor saves time here.
- Fry the grated potato in the minimum quantity of oil needed to prevent it sticking to the frying pan. Keep the pan covered with a lid but stir from time to time.
- The aim is to keep the fried potato moist, not dry and crisp.
- Cook until soft (10–15 minutes depending on the heat).
- Cut the corned beef into thin slices and dip each slice in beaten egg before frying slowly in a separate pan, again with the minimum of oil.
- Serve hot from the pan.

Bubble and Squeak

This traditional lunch or supper dish makes excellent use of odds and ends of potato, vegetables and meat, all bound together with an egg and fried.

Quantities are not important, provided that there is some variety.

All the ingredients, except for the egg, should have been cooked beforehand.

leftover cooked potatoes, meat, vegetables	1 egg per person

- Dice the cold meat and vegetables.
- Allow 1 egg per person. Beat the eggs and then stir them into the cold meat and vegetables.
- Fry over a moderate heat for 10–15 minutes, turning after 5 minutes.
- Sprinkle with grated cheese and brown the top under the grill before serving.
- If you have insufficient leftovers for bubble and squeak, make them into a soup with the addition of lentils to thicken it. See the Soups section.

Falafel

A traditional Middle Eastern snack, usually deep fried in oil, and without the egg. This method ensures the chickpeas are properly cooked.

SERVES 4

8 oz or 225 g of dried chickpeas	1 teaspoon ground cumin
1 medium onion, peeled and chopped	1 teaspoon ground coriander
	pinch of salt
4 cloves of garlic, peeled and crushed	2 tablespoons olive oil
	½ teaspoon bicarbonate of soda
fresh parsley or coriander, 2 heaped tablespoons when chopped	½ teaspoon cream of tartar
	1 egg

- Soak the chickpeas in plenty of water for 24 hours before use, then rinse in fresh water.
- Boil the chickpeas vigorously for 10 minutes and use a slotted spoon to remove any scum or foam from the water.
- Simmer the chickpeas in fresh water for 1 hour, then drain.
- In a food processor, grind the chickpeas and onion to a coarse purée.
- Mix in all the remaining ingredients.
- Spoon the mixture in walnut sized balls onto an oiled baking tray and flatten slightly.
- Bake in a preheated oven, gas mark 6, 400°F, 200°C for 15–20 minutes or until golden brown.
- Serve hot as a snack or starter.

Savoury Ducks or Faggots

Purchased savoury ducks often contain gluten.

SERVES 4

12 oz or 325 g pigs' liver, well chopped
4 oz or 100 g pig fat or lard
1 large, well-chopped onion
salt to taste
fresh ground black pepper to taste

pinch herbs: sage, thyme, basil
pinch grated nutmeg to taste
1 egg
12 oz or 325 g gluten-free breadcrumbs
8 rashers bacon

- Place all the ingredients except for the egg, bacon and breadcrumbs in a pan. Cover with a tight-fitting lid and cook gently for 30 minutes.
- Pour off the fat and allow the mixture to cool slightly.
- Beat the egg and stir this into the mixture.
- Stir gluten-free breadcrumbs into the mixture until it becomes stiff.
- Form the mixture into egg-sized lumps, wrap a slice of bacon round each lump and place on a baking tray.
- Bake in a preheated oven, gas mark 4, 350°F, 180°C, for 12–15 minutes, until the bacon is cooked.

Starters

Avocado and Cheese

MAKES 2 PORTIONS

1 ripe avocado
salt to taste
lemon juice to taste

1 oz or 25 g cottage cheese
1 oz or 25 g grated Cheddar
cheese

- Mash the flesh of the avocado with the salt and lemon juice.
- Place the cottage cheese as the bottom layer in a ramekin.
- Cover the cottage cheese with the avocado.
- Place the grated Cheddar cheese on top.
- Grill until the Cheddar cheese has melted and serve hot in the ramekin.

Deep-fried Mushrooms

SERVES 4

8 oz or 225 g button mushrooms
oil for cooking

For the batter

1 egg
2 tablespoons milk or water
½ large banana
2 oz or 50 g gluten-free flour mix

pinch salt to taste
¼ teaspoon bicarbonate of soda
¼ teaspoon cream of tartar

- Beat the banana to a purée with the egg and milk. This is best done in a liquidiser.
- Mix all the dry ingredients together.
- Fold the dry ingredients into the purée to make a sticky batter.
- Dip the mushrooms individually in the batter to coat them and lower them gently into the oil.

- Fry until golden brown
- Drain on absorbent kitchen paper briefly before serving.
- Serve immediately as the batter will soon lose its crispness.
- Serve with a hot cheese or a tomato sauce.

Variations
- Use 2 oz/50 g grated apple or 2 oz/50 g tofu in place of banana.

Grilled Grapefruit

PER PERSON

½ *grapefruit*   *brown sugar to taste*
cinnamon to taste

- Place the grapefruit halves, cut side up, in a bun tray.
- Dust the top with cinnamon and brown sugar.
- Grill under a gentle heat until hot.
- Serve in a bowl or a ramekin.

Soups

Do not use stock cubes unless you are sure they do not contain gluten.

Beef Stock

2 lb or 1 kg beef marrowbones	1 bay leaf
2 pints or 1 litre water	4 black peppercorns, whole
1 sliced onion	salt to taste
1 sliced carrot	

- Place the bones and water in a pressure cooker and simmer gently for 15 minutes. Remove any scum that forms on the surface.
- Add the remaining ingredients and cook under 15 lb pressure for 45 minutes. Cool.
- Without a pressure cooker simmer gently for 4 hours.
- Strain the stock and leave to go cold. Then remove the solid fat from the surface
- Freeze the stock in small quantities for later use in soups, stews and sauces.
- Use the fat for making crispbread.

Chicken Stock

- Follow the same recipe using the chicken carcass or 10 oz/300 g chicken giblets.

Fish Stock

- Follow the same recipe using 1 lb/450 g fish trimmings.

Cauliflower and Cheese Soup

Do not use stock cubes until you are sure they do not contain gluten.

SERVES 4

1 onion
½ cauliflower
½ pint or 280 ml water or chicken
  stock
pinch thyme
pinch salt to taste

pinch fresh ground pepper
1 teaspoon cornflour
½ pint or 280 ml milk
4 oz or 100 g hard cheese or
  fromage frais

- Cook the onion and cauliflower in the water until soft, together with the thyme, salt and fresh ground pepper. Mash these up with a potato masher or use a food processor.
- Add a little cold milk to the cornflour and mix into a paste, then add the rest of the milk. Stir these into the vegetables.
- Stir in the grated cheese or fromage frais, heating the soup until hot enough to serve but not boiling.
- This should be a fairly thick soup.
- Serve with thin slices of toasted banana bread as a lunch dish.

Tomato and Apple Soup

Do not use stock cubes unless you are sure they do not contain gluten.

SERVES 4

4 oz or 100 g well-chopped
  onions
2 oz or 50 g butter
6 oz or 175 g chopped tomatoes
6 oz or 175 g chopped apples
¼ pint or 150 ml red wine

salt to taste
¼ teaspoon fresh ground black
  pepper
1 pint or 550 ml chicken stock

- Cook the onions slowly in the butter for 10 minutes.
- Add the rest of the ingredients except for the stock and simmer gently in the wine for 1 hour in a pan with a tight-fitting lid.
- Liquidise the contents of the pan and then add the stock and stir well while reheating.
- Serve in warm soup bowls. Garnish with thin sliced eating apple.

Bean Soup

Do not use stock cubes unless you are sure they do not contain gluten.

SERVES 4

1 oz or 25 g haricot beans
1 oz or 25 g mung beans
1 oz or 25 g azuki beans
4 oz or 100 g well-chopped
  onions

1 oz or 25 g butter or oil
salt to taste
fresh ground black pepper to taste
1 pint of 550 ml chicken stock or
  other stock

- Soak the beans in 1 pint water overnight. Discard the water and rinse the beans.
- Cook the onions slowly in the butter or oil for 10 minutes.
- Add the rest of the ingredients including the beans and the stock.
- Bring to the boil and boil rapidly for 10 minutes.

- Then simmer gently for 1½ hours.
- Serve in warm soup bowls. Garnish with chopped parsley.

Tapioca Soup

Do not use stock cubes unless you are sure they do not contain gluten.

SERVES 4

*4 oz or 100 g well-chopped
  onions
2 oz or 50 g chopped carrots
2 oz or 50 g chopped celery
1 oz or 25 g butter or oil
1 pint or 550 ml stock*

*salt to taste
fresh ground black pepper to taste
2 oz or 50 g pearl tapioca
¼ pint or 150 ml milk
2 egg yolks*

- Cook the onions, carrots and celery slowly in the butter or oil for 10 minutes. Add the stock, salt and pepper and sprinkle in the tapioca. Bring to the boil and simmer gently for 40 minutes.
- Allow to cool slightly and then liquidise.
- Beat the yolks with the cold milk and stir into the cooled soup.
- Continue to stir as you bring the soup back to the boil before serving.
- Serve in warm soup bowls.

Scotch Broth

Do not use stock cubes unless you are sure they do not contain gluten. Do not use barley.

SERVES 4

1 pint or 550 ml mutton stock
2 oz or 50 g well-chopped onions
2 oz or 50 g leeks, cut into rings
2 oz or 50 g thinly sliced carrots
2 oz or 50 g chopped turnip or
  swede

2 oz or 50 g chopped potatoes
1 oz or 25 g long grain rice
salt to taste
fresh ground black pepper

- Add all the ingredients to the stock. Bring to the boil and simmer gently for 1 hour.
- Serve in warm soup bowls. Garnish with chopped parsley.

Leek and Potato Soup

Do not use stock cubes unless you are sure they do not contain gluten.

SERVES 4

1 pint or 550 ml stock
4 oz or 100 g well-chopped
  onions
4 oz or 100 g leeks, cut into rings
8 oz or 225 g chopped potatoes

1 oz or 25 g butter or oil
salt to taste
fresh ground black pepper to
taste

- Cook the onions and leeks slowly in the butter or oil for 10 minutes.
- Add the rest of the ingredients and the stock.
- Bring to the boil and simmer gently for 40 minutes.
- Allow to cool slightly and then liquidise.
- Bring back to the boil before serving.
- Serve in warm soup bowls. Garnish with chopped chives.

Bacon and Lentil Soup

Do not use stock cubes unless you are sure they do not contain gluten.

SERVES 4

1 knuckle of bacon
4 oz or 100 g well-chopped onions
1 oz or 25 g butter or oil
4 oz or 100 g diced carrot and swede

4 oz or 100 g red lentils
¼ teaspoon fresh ground black pepper
Do not add salt

- Soak the knuckle of bacon overnight in cold water (enough to cover), and then bring to the boil.
- **Discard that water**. Remove and discard the bacon skin.
- Cover the knuckle with fresh water.
- Cook the onions slowly in the butter or oil for 10 minutes
- Add the onions and the rest of the ingredients to the knuckle.
- Bring to the boil and simmer gently for 1½ hours, or pressure cook for 30 minutes.
- Serve in warm soup bowls. Garnish with crisp fried bacon.

Black Mushroom Soup

Do not use stock cubes unless you are sure they do not contain gluten.

SERVES 4

4 oz or 100 g well-chopped onions	fresh ground black pepper
2 cloves garlic, crushed	1 pint or 550 ml stock
8 oz or 225 g flat mushrooms	¼ pint or 150 ml milk
1 oz or 25 g butter or oil	1 oz or 25 g cornflour
salt to taste	

- Cook the onions, mushrooms and garlic slowly in the butter or oil for 10 minutes.
- Add the salt, pepper and the stock.
- Bring to the boil and simmer gently for 40 minutes.
- Allow to cool slightly and then liquidise.
- Bring back to the boil.
- Mix the cornflour with the cold milk before stirring into the soup.
- Stir the soup as it simmers for a further 5 minutes.
- Serve in warm soup bowls. Garnish with thinly sliced button mushrooms.

Carrot Soup

Do not use stock cubes unless you are sure they do not contain gluten.

SERVES 4

4 oz or 100 g well-chopped
  onions
4 oz or 100 g chopped turnip or
  swede
8 oz or 225 g chopped carrot
1 oz or 25 g butter or oil

salt to taste
fresh ground black pepper to
  taste
1 pint or 550 ml stock
¼ pint or 150 ml milk

- Cook the onions, carrots and swede slowly in the butter or oil for 10 minutes.
- Add the salt, pepper and the stock.
- Bring to the boil and simmer gently for 40 minutes.
- Allow to cool slightly and then liquidise.
- Bring back to the boil and stir in the milk before serving.
- Serve in warm soup bowls. Garnish with grated carrot.

Variations
- Use beetroot in place of carrot.
- Use leeks in place of onion.
- Use marrow in place of swede.

Meat and poultry

Beef Stew

Do not use stock cubes unless you are sure they do not contain gluten.

SERVES 4

1 lb or 450 g shin of beef
1 tablespoon olive oil
1 large onion
1 oz or 25 g mushrooms
6 oz or 175 g carrots
1 oz or 25 g cornflour or rice
flour

½ pint or 280 ml beef stock
salt to taste
¼ teaspoon fresh ground black
pepper
1 bayleaf

- Cut the beef into bite-sized cubes and then brown in a hot frying pan with a little oil.
- Chop and then briefly fry the onion, mushroom and carrot.
- Mix the flour to a paste with a small amount of the *cold* stock and then continue to stir as you add the rest of the stock to it.
- Place the beef and onion with the stock in a casserole.
- Add the herbs and seasoning.
- Bring to a simmer over a low heat.
- Cover with a tight-fitting lid and cook slowly in the oven, gas mark 1, 275°F, 140°C, for 3 hours.
- Check at intervals to make sure it is simmering gently and add more water if required.

Beefburgers

SERVES 4

8 oz or 225 g potato	mixed dried herbs
1 onion	salt to taste
2 oz or 50 g pea flour	1 lb or 450 g minced beef
1 egg	

- Cook the potato and onion together in water until soft, then drain and mash well.
- Beat together the egg, flour, herbs and salt.
- Mix in the minced beef and potato.
- Sprinkle a little of the pea flour on a tray and spoon out the mixture onto the flour. Flatten the mixture for beefburgers, or roll into sausage shapes.
- Fry in fat or oil, or grill, turning to cook both sides, until brown.
- Serve with egg and chips.

Variation
- use savoury gluten-free flour mix in place of pea flour.

Turkeyburgers

SERVES 4

12 oz or 325 g minced turkey	herbs to taste
4 oz or 100 g minced belly pork	salt to taste
rice flour	

- Use a food processor to blend the ingredients together.
- Spoon the mixture onto a tray dusted with rice flour.
- Fry in fat or oil, turning to cook both sides, until brown.

Turkey in Stilton Sauce and Rice Noodles

SERVES 2

2 oz or 50 g chopped mushrooms
1 chopped small onion
1 tablespoon olive oil
4 oz or 100 g cooked turkey meat
2 fl oz or 60 ml single cream
2 fl oz or 60 ml milk

1 oz or 25 g Stilton cheese
salt to taste
2 oz or 50 g rice noodles
1 oz or 25 g grated Cheddar
 cheese

- Fry the chopped mushroom and onion together until soft, then add bite-sized pieces of cooked turkey and cover with the cream and milk.
- Crumble in the Stilton cheese and bring to a gentle simmer.
- If the sauce seems too thick then stir in a little more milk.
- Cover the rice noodles with water in a separate pan and simmer for 5 minutes until soft.
- Drain the rice noodles and place half in a casserole.
- Pour the turkey and Stilton mixture onto the rice noodles in the casserole, then add the remaining noodles.
- Sprinkle the grated Cheddar cheese on top.
- Bake in a preheated oven, gas mark 4, 350°F, 180°C, for 12–15 minutes.

Chilli Con Carne

SERVES 4

4 oz or 100 g red kidney beans
1 onion, coarsely chopped
1 clove garlic, crushed
2 tablespoons olive oil
1 lb or 450 g minced beef
8 oz or 225 g tomatoes
2 oz or 50 g green pepper
½ pint or 280 ml water

1 teaspoon chilli powder
1 teaspoon cumin powder
1 teaspoon chopped oregano
2 bay leaves
1 teaspoon chopped parsley
salt to taste

- Soak the kidney beans overnight in 2 pints water. Discard the water, then boil vigorously for at least 30 minutes in fresh water. Discard the water and then continue to **boil** in 1 pint fresh water for 1 hour until tender. (Or use tinned kidney beans.)
- Fry the onion and garlic in the olive oil until soft.
- Add the minced beef and fry until brown.
- Add the remaining ingredients, except the kidney beans, and simmer gently in ½ pint water for 20 minutes to 1 hour. Then drain the cooked kidney beans, add them to the meat and simmer for a further 30 minutes before serving.
- Serve with rice and a side salad.

Roasting Meat

- Place the meat in a roasting tin on the middle shelf of a hot oven, gas mark 7, 425°F, 220°C.
- After 20 minutes turn the heat down to moderately hot, gas mark 5, 375°F, 190°C.
- If the meat does not have its own layer of fat on top then baste the joint with hot dripping at intervals or place an extra strip of fat over the joint while it is cooking.
- For beef on the bone allow a total cooking time of 15 minutes per lb/450 g and 15 minutes extra.
- For beef without a bone and for lamb or mutton allow a total cooking time of 20 minutes per lb/450 g and 20 minutes extra.
- For pork or veal allow a total cooking time of 25 minutes per lb/450 g and 25 minutes extra.
- Allow the joint to stand in a warm place for 10–15 minutes before serving.
- Less tender meat can be roasted at a lower temperature, gas mark 4, 350°F, 180°C.
- Allow a total cooking time of 35 minutes per lb/450 g and 35 minutes extra.
- Less tender meat can be pot-roasted. The meat should be placed in a saucepan with a tight-fitting lid. Sufficient dripping or lard should be placed with the meat and it should be fried, turning until browned all over.
- The heat should then be reduced and the lid put in place, to simmer until cooked. Allow a total cooking time of 45 minutes per lb/450 g.

Roast Chicken

- The prepared chicken should be washed well in cold water both inside and out and allowed to drain. Any neck or giblets inside should be removed. Frozen chicken must be completely thawed before cooking starts.
- Place the meat in a roasting tin on the middle shelf of a hot oven, gas mark 7, 425°F, 200°C.
- After 20 minutes turn the heat down to moderately hot, gas mark 5, 375°F, 190°C.
- If the poultry does not have its own layer of fat on top then baste the joint with hot dripping at intervals or place an extra strip of fat, e.g. bacon, over the chicken while it is cooking.
- For chicken and duck allow a total cooking time of 15 minutes per lb/450 g and 15 minutes extra.
- To check to see if the bird is cooked, pull at the junction between the thigh joint and the body. If the juices here are clear and the meat at the joint starts to separate from the bone then the bird is cooked. If the juices here are still pink then cook for longer.
- The juices that run out of the body cavity should also be clear, not pink.
- Chicken is best cooked without being stuffed.
- Cook gluten-free stuffing on a separate tray. See page 80.

Roast Turkey

Allow 2–3 lb/0.9–1.3 kg turkey per person for a Christmas dinner. A family of four would need an oven-ready turkey weighing 8–12 lb/3.6–5.5 kg.

- The prepared turkey should be washed well in cold water both inside and out and allowed to drain. Any neck or giblets inside should be removed. Frozen turkey must be completely thawed before cooking starts.
- Rub the skin with butter and then season lightly with salt and pepper. Lay several rashers of fatty, streaky bacon to cover the breast, then cover the turkey with foil. This can form a good lid over the roasting tin, or the turkey can be placed on foil which is then folded and crimped over the top of the turkey.

- Place the turkey in a roasting tin on the middle shelf of a hot oven, gas mark 7, 425°F, 220°C.
- After 30 minutes turn the heat down to moderately hot, gas mark 3, 325°F, 160°C for 2½–3 hours.
- Then turn the heat up to gas mark 6, 400°F, 200°C, and remove the foil and bacon for the final 30 minutes.
- Baste the turkey with its own juices several times in this final 30 minutes.
- The cooked turkey should then be allowed to relax in a warm place for 30 minutes before serving.
- To check to see if the bird is cooked run a skewer through the thickest thigh meat. The juice should be golden with no trace of pink. The juices that run out of the body cavity should also be clear, not pink.

We have a family of seven for Christmas and purchase a 14 lb/6.3 kg fresh turkey. This is cooked for 40 minutes at the initial high temperature, for 3½ hours at the lower temperature and then 40 minutes for the final crisping of the skin without foil.

Stuffing

SERVES 4

8 oz or 225 g minced pork
2 oz or 50 g chopped onion
2 oz or 50 g gluten-free
  breadcrumbs
salt to taste

fresh ground black pepper to
  taste
2 teaspoons herbs to taste: sage,
  thyme

- Mix all the ingredients together.
- If cooked separately from the bird, place in a baking tray beside the roasting bird for the last 30–40 minutes.

Irish Stew

SERVES 4

1 lb or 450 g stewing mutton
1 lb or 450 g potatoes
4 oz or 100 g chopped onion
4 oz or 100 g chopped carrot
4 oz or 100 g chopped swede

1 oz or 25 g cornflour
½ pint or 280 ml water
salt to taste
fresh ground black pepper

- Trim any lumps of visible fat from the meat, then cut meat into bite-sized chunks.
- Scrub and slice the potatoes and place half as a layer on the bottom of a stewing pan.
- Cover with the meat, then the carrot and swede, then the onion and finally the remaining potato on top.
- Mix the cornflour with a small amount of cold water to form a paste.
- Sprinkle with the salt and pepper and add the water and cornflour to the stew.
- Bring to the boil and cover with a lid and simmer gently for at least 1½ hours, adding more water if necessary.
- Irish stew can also be cooked slowly in the oven, gas mark 5, 375°F, 190°C for 30 minutes to boil the stew and then, gas mark 2, 300°F, 150°C for 1 hour.

Steak and Kidney Pie

SERVES 4

1 lb prepared shortcrust pastry.
  See page 166 for ingredients.
1 lb or 450 g stewing steak
6 oz or 175 g ox kidney
2 oz or 50 g pea flour or gram
  flour

4 oz or 100 g chopped onion
½ pint or 280 ml water
salt to taste
fresh ground black pepper to
  taste

- Take two-thirds of the prepared pastry, roll it and use it to line a 1½ pint pie dish. Roll the remaining pastry and put to one side for the top.
- Cook the empty pastry shell in the pie dish for 15–20 minutes or until brown in a preheated oven, gas mark 7, 425°F, 220°C.
- Cut the steak and the kidney into bite-sized chunks and roll them in the flour. Fry them in a little oil together with the chopped onion, then add the water and simmer gently for about 1 hour until the meat is tender.
- Place the hot, cooked meat and onion in the pastry-lined dish.
- Brush the edge of the dish with water, place the pastry over the dish and press down to seal the edges.
- Bake in a preheated oven, gas mark 6, 400°F, 200°C, for 20 minutes or until the pastry on top is cooked.

Chicken and Stilton

PER PERSON

1 chicken breast
1 oz or 25 g blue Stilton cheese
or Gruyère cheese

1 rasher of bacon, streaky is best
white wine as required

- Roll the Stilton inside the chicken breast and then roll this inside the bacon.
- Pin this together with a cocktail stick.
- Sit it in an ovenproof dish with the flap of bacon underneath to stop it unrolling.
- Now pour a little white wine over the roll.
- Leave to marinade for 4 hours, basting with the wine at intervals.
- Bake in a preheated oven, gas mark 6, 400°F, 200°C, for 40 minutes to 1 hour, depending on thickness.
- Serve hot, garnishing each plate with lettuce, tomato and cucumber. This dish is also very good served cold.

Variations
- Use half a chicken breast per person and serve as the starter.

Chicken Hotpot

Serves 4

1 lb or 450 g chicken joints	14 oz or 400 g tinned tomatoes
1 oz or 25 g lentil flour or gram flour	2 cloves garlic crushed, or to taste
1 tablespoon olive oil	1 oz or 25 g lentils
4 oz or 100 g chopped onion	1 teaspoon dried mixed herbs
4 oz or 100 g chopped carrot or parsnip	½ pint or 280 ml chicken stock or water
4 oz or 100 g chopped swede or turnip	salt to taste
8 oz or 225 g mushrooms	fresh ground black pepper to taste

- Remove the skin from the joints and roll the joints in lentil flour.
- Fry the joints gently in oil until browned on both sides and then place in a casserole.
- Chop and then fry the onion until translucent and then add to the casserole.
- Add the chopped carrot, swede, parsnip and turnip together with the mushrooms, tinned tomatoes, crushed garlic, mixed herbs and lentils.
- Sprinkle with the salt and pepper and add just enough water or chicken stock to cover.
- Cook in a preheated oven, gas mark 5, 375"F, 190"C for 30 minutes to boil the casserole, and then gas mark 2, 300°F, 150°C for 1 hour.
- Alternatively cook in a pressure cooker under 15 lb (high) pressure for 20 minutes.

Chicken and Rice Pot Roast

SERVES 4 TO 6

3 lb or 1.2 kg roasting chicken
1 oz or 25 g butter
1 chopped onion
8 oz or 225 g brown rice
1 chopped red pepper
4 oz or 100 g mushrooms
1 tablespoon tomato purée

1 pint or 550 ml chicken stock
(gluten-free)
1 bay leaf
2 oz or 50 g frozen peas
1 small can sweet corn
salt and pepper to taste
parsley to garnish

- Rub the butter over the chicken and place in a roasting tin on the middle shelf of a hot oven gas mark 7, 425°F, 200°C for 20 minutes or until brown.
- Remove the chicken and fry the onions in the butter until soft.
- Place the rice in a large roasting pot with a lid. Pour the butter, juices and the onion onto the rice, and stir to mix well.
- Add the chopped red pepper, mushrooms, tomato purée, gluten-free chicken stock, seasoning and the bay leaf.
- Place the browned chicken in the roasting pot with these ingredients and cover.
- Cook for 1¼ hours, gas mark 5, 375°F, 190°C.
- Then add the peas and sweet corn. Stir these into the rice.
- Return to the oven for 15 minutes until the chicken is fully cooked.

Chicken Kiev

SERVES 2

2 oz or 50 g butter or margarine
chopped parsley
1 clove garlic, chopped
2 boned and skinned chicken
  breasts

2 oz or 50 g cornflakes
1 egg, beaten
oil for frying

- Mix the butter, garlic and parsley into a paste.
- Slice each chicken breast deeply from the side but don't cut right through.
- Spread the butter paste between the flaps of the chicken breast and then use cocktail sticks to hold the flaps together.
- Crush the cornflakes to a fine powder inside a plastic bag.
- Dip the chicken in the beaten egg and then into the crushed cornflakes until they are fully coated.
- Fry the chicken portions in oil on a medium heat for 25–30 minutes or until they are a golden colour and cooked through.

Tangy Liver

SERVES 4

1 lb or 450 g ox liver
4 tomatoes, quartered
1 onion, chopped
herbs – rosemary, thyme, oregano

1 orange
4 oz or 100 g mushrooms
olive oil to fry onions

- Fry gently the onion in the olive oil until translucent.
- Add the mushrooms and fry for a further 2 minutes.
- Add the liver cut into strips. Fry quickly, turning until sealed.
- Add the orange juice and rind.
- Add the tomatoes and fry just long enough to heat through.
- Sprinkle with herbs.

Chinese chicken

SERVES 2

2 chicken breasts

For the marinade:
piece of root ginger
pinch salt
pinch black pepper
  1 teaspoon sugar

1 teaspoon cornflour
2 teaspoons dry sherry
2 tablespoons olive oil

For the sauce
2 tablespoons olive oil
1 medium carrot, peeled and
  sliced thinly
2 cloves garlic, peeled and
  crushed
2 shallots, peeled and sliced
½ teaspoon sesame oil

2 slices root ginger
3 oz or 75 g canned bamboo
  shoots, sliced
2 fl oz or 60 ml chicken stock
2 teaspoons cornflour dissolved
in 2 tablespoons of cold water

- Slice and liquidise the root ginger (reserve 2 slices for the sauce).
- Extract the ginger juice and discard the fibre.
- Cut the chicken into thin slices.
- Mix the sliced chicken with the ginger juice, 1 teaspoon cornflour, salt, pepper and sherry and leave to marinade for 30 minutes.
- Fry the chicken in oil until almost cooked, then put to one side.
- Add another two tablespoons of oil to the pan. Add the carrot, garlic, shallots, slices of ginger and sesame oil and simmer gently until the carrot is almost cooked and the shallots translucent.
- Add the stock, 2 teaspoons cornflour dissolved in 2 tablespoons of cold water, the sliced bamboo shoots and the chicken.
- Simmer and stir until the sauce thickens and the chicken is cooked.
- Serve hot with rice.

Curry and hot spice mixtures

Hot spice mixtures can be added to stews, used as a marinade before grilling, or added to vegetable dishes. Blending your own curry powder allows you to select the strength and balance of flavours that suit you. The best flavour comes from dry roasting the whole spices, before grinding when cool. Using ready ground spices makes the whole process much quicker.

3 dried red chillies, with the seeds removed and discarded	*1 teaspoon mustard seeds*
1 teaspoon coriander seeds	*1 teaspoon black peppercorns*
1 teaspoon cumin seeds	*1 teaspoon ground turmeric*
1 teaspoon fenugreek seeds	*1 teaspoon ground ginger*

- Place the whole spices in a pan and dry roast over a moderate heat. Keep the pieces moving all the time until they darken
- Allow the spices to cool and then grind into a powder.
- Blend the freshly ground spices with the pre-ground spices.
- The curry powder is now ready to use.

Variations
- You can vary the proportion of all the ingredients to suit your own tastes.
- Other ingredients you can add are one or more of the following selection:
  1 teaspoon fennel seeds
  1 teaspoon nigella seeds
  2 stalks of lemon grass
  1 teaspoon cayenne pepper
  ¼ teaspoon ground asfoetida
  1 teaspoon caraway seeds (often added to Arabic spice blends)

Mild Curry Powder – Garam Masala

2 fresh bay leaves
1 teaspoon cumin seeds
1 teaspoon coriander seeds
1 teaspoon cardamom seeds
  (green or black)
1 teaspoon black peppercorns

1 teaspoon cloves
1 teaspoon ground mace
1 teaspoon ground cinnamon
  (You can use cinnamon sticks
  but they are difficult to grind.)

- Place the whole spices in a pan and dry roast over a moderate heat. Keep the spices moving all the time until they darken.
- Allow the spices to cool and then grind into a powder.
- Blend the freshly ground spices with the pre-ground spices.
- The curry powder is now ready to use – but don't add too much.

Variations
- Other ingredients you can add are: 1 teaspoon ajowan seeds, 1 tablespoon sesame seeds, ¼ teaspoon grated nutmeg.

Sweet and Sour Sauce

Meat or vegetables can be marinaded and cooked in the sauce, or the sauce can be made separately and served with the meat or vegetables.

1 medium onion, peeled and
  chopped
2 cloves of garlic, peeled and
  crushed
1 teaspoon mustard seeds
½ teaspoon ground ginger

2 tablespoons of olive oil
2 teaspoons cornflour
¼ pint or 150 ml cold water
1 tablespoon redcurrant jelly
1 or 2 tablespoons of wine
  vinegar.

- Simmer the onion, garlic, mustard seed and ginger in the olive oil until the onion is tender.
- Make the cornflour into a paste with a little of the cold water, then add the rest of the cold water and add to the onion.
- Continue to simmer gently until the sauce becomes translucent.
- Add the redcurrant jelly and the wine vinegar and stir well.
- Simmer before serving. Add a little more water if the sauce is too thick.

Sausages

Sausages are easy to make at home with equipment to fill the mixture into the skins. I have used the International King Chef Sausage Maker from Wrightway Marketing Ltd. Skins are available from good kitchen shops or by mail order from the same firm.

Cereals and binders are not necessary to produce a good sausage as fresh meat binds together very easily. However, rice flour and an egg can be added to the sausage mix if this is desired.

Man-made skins, or casings, are easiest to use and do not require any washing or soaking.

Natural skins are stronger and produce a gently curved sausage but need to be soaked to soften them before they are filled.

Sausages need a fairly high fat content in order to remain moist while cooking. This can be added to the mixture in the form of pig's back fat or fresh beef suet (not packet suet), or minced belly pork can be used.

These sausages contain no preservatives and should be used fresh. Sausages can be frozen until required for use provided they have been made with fresh ingredients.

Pork Sausages

MAKES 1 LB

1 lb or 450 g minced pork
2 teaspoons fresh mixed herbs:
  sage, thyme, rosemary
  or

1 teaspoon dried mixed herbs
salt and fresh ground pepper to
  taste
½ teaspoon allspice

- Beat the herbs and spices into the minced pork with the back of a spoon until it sticks into a ball, or use a food processor to blend the ingredients together.
- Fill the barrel of the sausage maker with this mixture.
- Cut a 1½ inch/4 cm length of compacted wide casing and fit this over the nozzle of the sausage maker. Tie a knot in the open end.
- Operate the sausage maker to extrude the mixture as a paste into

the skins, refilling the sausage maker as required. Do not overfill the skins.

- Tie knots in the open end of the skins and then twist the sausage at intervals to produce individual sausages. These are best not cut apart until after they have been cooked.
- Sausages should not be pricked and should be cooked slowly.
- Bake in a preheated oven, gas mark 4, 350°F, 180°C, for 30–40 minutes, or grill under a medium heat for 20–25 minutes, turning them at intervals to allow even cooking.
- Alternatively, fry them over a low heat for 20–25 minutes, turning them at intervals to allow even cooking.

Sausage Variations

BEEF AND TOMATO SAUSAGES

MAKES 1 LB

12 oz or 325 g minced beef
4 oz or 100 g minced belly pork
1 tablespoon tomato purée
2 teaspoon fresh herbs
   or

1 teaspoon dried mixed herbs
salt and pepper to taste

TURKEY AND GARLIC SAUSAGES

MAKES 1 LB

12 oz or 325 g minced turkey
4 oz or 100 g minced belly pork
2 cloves fresh garlic, grated
2 teaspoons fresh herbs
   or

1 teaspoon dried mixed herbs
salt and pepper to taste

Chipolata sausages

Makes 1 lb

12 oz or 325 g minced pork	1 small pinch each coriander,
4 oz or 100 g minced belly pork	pimento, grated nutmeg, thyme
1 oz or 25 g rice flour	salt and pepper to taste.
2 fl oz or 50 ml water	

Use the smaller chipolata skins for this sausage.

Pork and apple sausages

Makes 1 lb

10 oz or 275 g minced pork	1 teaspoon dried mixed herbs
4 oz or 100 g minced belly pork	salt and pepper to taste
4 oz or 100 g cooking apple	
2 teaspoons fresh herbs	
or	

Sausage Rolls

- Prepare long narrow sausages, the length of your baking tray, or roll the sausage meat to shape without skins.
- Prepare 8 oz/225 g pastry for each 1 lb/450 g sausages.
- Roll the gluten-free pastry of your choice to the same length as the sausage, roll the pastry round the sausage and place on the tray.
- Cut with a sharp knife into sausage roll lengths but do not move them.
- Bake at gas mark 5, 375°F, 190°C, for 40–45 minutes.

Fish

The fish should be gutted, cleaned and washed well in cold water and then drained. Skin with large prominent scales should be removed.

Baked Fish

METHOD 1
- Butter an ovenproof dish and lay the fish in the dish.
- Add one tablespoon of white wine or fish stock for each portion of fish.
- Rub a little butter over the upper surface of the fish.
- Cover the dish with foil.
- Bake in a preheated oven, gas mark 4, 350°F, 180°C, until cooked, depending on thickness: 8–12 minutes for thin fillets 15–20 minutes for small whole fish or thicker fillets; 25–30 minutes for whole large fish.
- The fish is cooked when the thickest flesh is translucent all the way through.

METHOD 2
- Take a piece of foil large enough to enclose the fish.
- Butter the foil, place the fish in the middle and cover the fish with dabs of butter, herbs and seasoning.
- Fold the foil to seal above the fish.
- Bake in a preheated oven, gas mark 5, 375°F, 190°C, until cooked, depending on thickness: 8–12 minutes for thin fillets; 15–20 minutes for small whole fish or thicker fillets; 25–30 minutes for whole large fish.

Herrings Baked in Foil

PER PERSON

1 herring
gluten-free wholegrain mustard

lentil flour, gram flour or
  sorghum flour

- Clean and wash the herring.
- Roll it in lentil or sorghum flour.
- Spread the cavity of the herring with wholegrain mustard.
- Take a piece of foil large enough to enclose the fish.
- Place the fish in the middle and fold the foil to seal above the fish.
- Bake in a preheated oven, gas mark 5, 375°F, 190°C, for 15–20 minutes until cooked, depending on thickness.
- The fish is cooked when the thickest flesh comes away from the bone.

Variations
- Fill the body cavity with gooseberries and fennel
- Cook mackerel in the same way.

Grilled Fish

Most types of round fish grill well but white fish fillets tend to dry out.
- Grill briefly under a fierce heat to crisp the skin but then reduce the heat to medium and grill more slowly until cooked.
- Cooking time depends on the thickness of the fish.
- Allow 6 minutes each side for a small fish and up to 10 minutes each side for a larger fish.
- Always watch the fish cooking and remove from the grill as soon as the thickest flesh comes away from the bone. It is easy to overcook grilled fish.

Grilled Trout

PER PERSON

1 trout   flaked almonds
butter or garlic butter

- Clean and wash the trout.
- Score the deepest flesh diagonally and rub butter into the skin.
- Grill briefly under a fierce heat to crisp the skin but then reduce the heat to medium and grill more slowly until cooked.
- Cooking time depends on the thickness of the trout.
- Allow 6 minutes each side for a small trout and up to 10 minutes each side for a larger trout.
- The trout is cooked when the thickest flesh comes away from the bone.
- Sprinkle with flaked almonds for the last 2 minutes under the grill.

Paella

SERVES 4

8 oz or 225 g rice   2 oz or 50 g tuna or salmon
1 large onion   4 oz or 100 g prepared prawns
pinch fresh herbs to taste   2 oz or 50 g shelled walnuts
salt to taste   2 oz or 50 g button mushrooms
8 oz or 225 g cod, haddock or   1 tin mussels in their shells
  coley

- Cook the rice until soft, together with the onions, herbs and salt.
- Cook the fish by steaming, and gently flake the fish when cooked.
- Keep some prawns and mussels to decorate the top.
- Mix all the ingredients together while hot, then cover and reheat in an oven for 30 minutes, gas mark 4, 350°F, 180°C.
- Decorate the top with prawns and mussels and serve with a side salad.

Deep-fried Fish

Most types of white fish fillets can be deep-fried as well as small whole fish, such as whitebait.

The fish should not be thicker than 1 inch/2.5 cm so that the fish and the batter cook in the same time.

Corn oil is a good oil to use as it will reach a high temperature without smoking.

Use a large, heavy chip pan and keep a close-fitting lid available in case of fire. Never fill the pan more than one-third full of oil.

FOR THE BATTER

1 egg	1 oz or 25 g dripping, lard or
4 fl oz or 125 ml milk or water	butter
2 oz or 50 g grated apple or tofu	pinch salt to taste
4 oz or 100 g gluten-free flour	½ teaspoon bicarbonate of soda
mix	¼ teaspoon cream of tartar

- Beat the apple/tofu to a purée with the egg and milk. This is best done in a liquidiser.
- Mix all the dry ingredients together and then rub in the fat.
- Fold the dry ingredients into the liquid ingredients to make a sticky batter.
- Heat the oil to 180–190°C/350–380°F.
- Use a fat thermometer or drop in a raw potato chip. If the temperature is correct it should bubble steadily.
- Dip the pieces of fish in the batter, ensuring that all the fish is covered and then lower gently into the hot oil.
- Do not put in more fish than you can see separately at the same time.
- Cook until golden brown.
- Lift the fish out with a perforated spoon and drain briefly before serving.
- Do not cook too long before serving as the batter may lose its crispness.

Poached Fish

Most types of fish can be cooked by poaching.
- Place the cleaned fish in a pan or ovenproof dish that fits the fish closely and cover it with cold water, milk, fish stock or white wine.
- Bring the liquid to a gentle boil, either in the oven or on the hob.
- Then reduce the heat so the liquid is just simmering, not boiling.
- Cooking time is taken from the start of boiling and depends on thickness: 8–12 minutes for thin fillets; 15–20 minutes for small whole fish or thicker fillets; 25–30 minute for whole large fish.
- The fish should be allowed to drain before serving.
- The liquid should be used in the preparation of a sauce.

Skate Wings

PER PERSON

skate wing, one small or ½ large   *herbs: fennel, rosemary, bay,*
milk   *basil*

- Choose a shallow pan with a lid in which all the skate wings can be placed in one layer without too much spare space.
- Lay the wings in the pan and add just sufficient milk to cover.
- Sprinkle with herbs and salt and pepper to taste.
- Bring to a simmer and cover with a lid.
- Simmer gently for 10–15 minutes depending on thickness. Turn after 5 minutes. When done the flesh lifts easily from the cartilage but the cartilage does not fall apart.
- Serve with black butter. See page 188 for recipe.
- Use the milk to make a sauce or fish soup (freeze until required).

Bread

Western-style bread has developed to make the most of the properties of wheat four. The wheat has also been selected over many years for improved bread making.

Do not expect any gluten-free bread to be an exact copy. You cannot make soft, moist, white bread without wheat flour.

There are many other ways of making bread. A wide variety of flours with better flavours and an improved nutritional balance is available.

Gluten-free breads are best served fresh and hot. These gluten-free breads do not go stale as quickly as wheat bread and they freeze well. Slice before freezing and serve by toasting slices straight from the freezer.

Gluten-free bread mixtures do not have the same texture as wheat flour doughs unless they contain banana *flour* which can absorb large quantities of water without becoming liquid.

Gluten-free bread mixtures need to be wet enough to make a thick batter, much moister than wheat flour dough. These mixtures cannot hold the CO_2 gas produced by yeast. Bicarbonate of soda and cream of tartar still need to be added to the mixture to help it rise.

The banana, carrot, apple, tofu or unsweetened tinned chestnut purée is an essential part of these recipes and should be beaten to a smooth purée with the milk and egg. This is best done in a liquidiser.

The flour mixture should then be folded into the purée with as little extra mixing as possible. The structure of the dough forms as the wet and dry ingredients are mixed together. Do not overmix as this will knock the gas out of the mixture and it will not raise the dough when it is cooked. Do not leave the wet dough to stand at this point or you will lose the light structure as the gas escapes. It must go straight into the oven to be cooked.

The sugar in these recipes reacts with the starch in cooking to improve the texture but makes the bread slightly sweet.

Gluten-free breads will seem drier, harder and have a darker texture than wheat bread. However, they have excellent nutritional value and offer you a variety of flavours.

Basic Bread

The secret of gluten-free bread is to use as many different sources of starch as possible. Try various combinations of flour to fit within your budget and your tastes.

Buckwheat flour bakes well but has a strong flavour. Some people find it indigestible. Sorghum and millet flours are excellent baking flours when combined with rice flour or gram flour. Sweet chestnut flour is also very useful in both bread and cake mixture and makes a softer bread. Teff is a very dark, nutty-flavoured flour. Mixtures including sorghum and sweet chestnut flours make the best bread and fruit cakes. Pea flours and gram flours should be used in moderation. A small amount improves flavour and nutrition but a large amount can give too strong a flavour and be indigestible.

In Africa and India a staple bread is produced by mixing sorghum, millet or white maize flour with boiling water to form a dough. The dough is then flattened by slapping from hand to hand, a skill that requires dexterity and practice. The flat loaves are cooked on a very hot ceramic or cast-iron surface, when they balloon up to give a light top and a heavy base. This method works only with very freshly ground flour.

The method of cooking makes a lot of difference to the bread. Cook the bread in a shallow basking tray rather than a bread tin. The batter should not be deeper than 1 inch/2.5 cm when poured into the tin. Cooking at gas mark 6, 400°F, 200°C, will produce a good crust but will dry out the bread in a fan oven.

Bread can be cooked at a lower temperature or it can be steamed for a much moister loaf. Always check that a loaf is cooked by using a skewer through the middle. The loaf is not cooked until the skewer comes out clean. A part-cooked loaf can be turned over on the baking tray to ensure even cooking.

Quick and Easy Flat Bread

This produces a tasty soft bread with a crisp golden crust.

MAKES ONE 1 LB LOAF

1 large banana	1 teaspoon bicarbonate of soda
1 egg	1 teaspoon cream of tartar
¼ pint or 150 ml milk	salt to taste
8 oz or 225 g gluten-free flour	2 tablespoons olive oil
mix	1 teaspoon sugar

- Beat the banana to a smooth purée with the milk and egg. This is best done in a liquidiser.
- Mix all the dry ingredients for the bread together with two tablespoons oil.
- Fold the flour mixture into the purée. Do not overmix and do not leave to stand at this point or you will lose the light structure to the bread dough.
- Line a 10 inch/25 cm square tray with non-stick baking parchment and spread the mixture in a 1 inch/2.5 cm deep layer in the tray, or in greased individual bun or pattie trays.
- Bake in a preheated oven, gas mark 7, 425°F, 220°C, for 35–40 minutes.
- Always check that a loaf is cooked by using a skewer through the middle. The loaf is not cooked until the skewer comes out clean. A part cooked loaf can be turned over on the baking tray to ensure even cooking.
- All gluten-free breads are best served fresh and hot. If bread is not being served immediately it is cooked, serve toasted.

Variations
- Use 4 oz/100 g grated carrot or 4 oz/100 g unsweetened chestnut purée or 4 oz/100 g tofu in place of the banana.

TOMATO BREAD
Add 1–4 teaspoons tomato purée to the liquidised mixture.

HERB BREAD
Add 1–4 teaspoons dried mixed herbs and several chopped olives to the flour mixture.

Carrot Flat Bread

This produces a tasty bread with a crisp brown crust.

MAKES ONE **1** LB LOAF

4 oz or 100 g grated carrot
1 egg
¼ pint or 150 ml milk
2 tablespoons olive oil
    or
4 oz or 100 g grated cheese
8 oz or 225 g gluten-free flour
    mix

1 oz or 25 g dried milk
1 teaspoon bicarbonate of soda
½ teaspoon cream of tartar
salt to taste
1 teaspoon sugar

- Beat the carrot to a smooth purée with the milk and egg. This is best done in a liquidiser.
- Mix all the dry ingredients for the bread together with two tablespoons oil or grated cheese.
- Fold the flour mixture into the purée. Do not overmix and do not leave to stand at this point or you will lose the light structure of the bread dough.
- Line a 10 inch/25 cm square shallow tray with non-stick baking parchment and spread the mixture in a 1 inch/2.5 cm deep layer in the tray, or use greased individual pattie tins.
- Bake in a preheated oven, gas mark 7, 425°F, 200°C for 35–45 minutes.
- Always check that a loaf is cooked by using a skewer through the middle. The loaf is not cooked until the skewer comes out clean.
- All gluten-free breads are best served fresh and hot. If bread is not being served immediately it is cooked, serve toasted.

Variations
- Use sorghum or millet flour in place of cornflour.

Potato Flat Bread

This produces a potato-flavoured bread with a crisp brown crust.

MAKES ONE 1 LB LOAF	
3 oz or 75 g potato	2 tablespoons olive oil
¼ pint or 150 ml milk	1 teaspoon bicarbonate of soda
1 egg	1 teaspoon cream of tartar
6 oz or 175 g gluten-free flour	salt to taste
mix	1 teaspoon sugar

- Cook the potato until soft and drain well. Mash the potato well or put through a liquidiser.
- Beat the milk and egg together with the cooked potato. This is best done in a liquidiser.
- Mix all the dry ingredients for the bread together with two tablespoons oil.
- Fold the flour mixture into the purée. Do not overmix and do not leave to stand at this point or you will lose the light structure to the bread dough.
- Line a 10 inch/25 cm square shallow tray with baking parchment and spread the mixture in a 1 inch/2.5 cm deep layer in the tray, or use individual greased pattie tins.
- Bake in a preheated oven, gas mark 7, 425°F, 220°C, for 35–45 minutes.
- Always check that a loaf is cooked by using a skewer through the middle. The loaf is not cooked until the skewer comes out clean. A part-cooked loaf can be turned over on the baking tray to ensure even cooking.

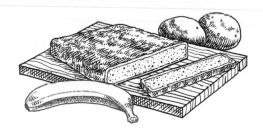

Allmeal Bread

Put all your containers of gluten-free flour in a row and take 1 or 2 tablespoons from each. There is no need to weigh all the ingredients! Just make sure the total weight of flour is close to 8 oz/225 g.

MAKES ONE 1 LB LOAF

1 small banana
4 oz or 100 g grated carrot
¼ pint or 150 ml water or milk
1 egg
8 oz or 225 g gluten-free
  flour

1 teaspoon bicarbonate of soda
½ teaspoon cream of tartar
salt to taste
1 oz or 25 g lard or 2
  tablespoons olive oil
1 teaspoon sugar

- Beat the banana and carrot to a smooth purée with the milk and egg. This is best done in a liquidiser.
- Mix all the dry ingredients for the bread together with two tablespoons oil.
- Fold the flour mixture into the purée. Do not overmix and do not leave to stand at this point or you will lose the light structure to the bread dough.
- Pour the batter, 1 inch/2.5 cm deep, into a shallow 10 inch/ 25 cm square baking tray lined with non-stick baking parchment.
- Bake in a preheated oven, gas mark 7, 425°F, 220°C, for 35–45 minutes.
- Always check that a loaf is cooked by using a skewer through the middle. The loaf is not cooked until the skewer comes out clean. A part-cooked loaf can be turned over on the baking tray to ensure even cooking.

Variations
- The best bread includes sorghum, sweet chestnut and teff flour.
- Use 4 oz or 100 g prunes in place of the banana.

Sorghum Bread

A dark-brown bread with a soft texture and mild flavour.

MAKES ONE 1 LB LOAF

¼ pint or 150 ml water or milk
1 or 2 eggs
1 small banana
4 oz or 100 g grated carrot
4 oz or 100 g sorghum flour
4 oz or 100 g rice flour

1 teaspoon bicarbonate of soda
½ teaspoon cream of tartar
salt to taste
1 oz or 25 g fat or 2 tablespoons
  olive oil

- See Buckwheat Bread for method.

Rice Bread

MAKES ONE 1 LB LOAF

1 large banana
4 oz or 100 g grated carrot
1 egg
¼ pint or 150 ml water or milk
4 oz or 100 g rice flour
4 oz or 100 g potato flour
1 oz or 25 g soya flour (optional)

1 teaspoon bicarbonate of soda
½ teaspoon cream of tartar
salt to taste
1 oz or 25 g fat or 2 tablespoons
  olive oil
1 teaspoon sugar

- Beat the banana and carrot to a smooth purée with the milk and egg. This is best done in a liquidiser.
- Mix all the dry ingredients for the bread together with one tablespoon oil.
- Fold the flour mixture into the purée. Do not overmix and do not leave to stand at this point or you will lose the light structure to the bread dough.
- Pour the batter, 1 inch/2.5 cm deep, into a shallow 10 inch/ 25 cm square baking tray lined with non-stick baking parchment.
- Bake in a preheated oven, gas mark 7, 425°F, 220°C, for 35–45 minutes.
- Always check that a loaf is cooked by using a skewer through the middle. The loaf is not cooked until the skewer comes out clean. A part-cooked loaf can be turned over on the baking tray to ensure even cooking.

Buckwheat Bread

A strong-flavoured bread.

MAKES ONE 1 LB LOAF

1 large banana
4 oz or 100 g grated carrot
¼ pint or 150 ml water or milk
1 egg
4 oz or 100 g buckwheat flour
4 oz or 100 g rice four

1 teaspoon bicarbonate of soda
salt to taste
1 oz or 25 g fat or 2 tablespoons
  olive oil
1 oz or 25 g sugar

- Beat the banana and carrot to a smooth purée with the milk and egg. This is best done in a liquidiser.
- Mix all the dry ingredients for the bread together with two tablespoons oil.
- Fold the flour mixture into the purée. Do not overmix and do not leave to stand at this point or you will lose the light structure to the bread dough.
- Place the sticky batter, 1 inch/2.5 cm deep, into a shallow 10 inch/25 cm square baking tray lined with non-stick baking parchment.
- Bake in a preheated oven, gas mark 7, 425°F, 220°C, for 35–45 minutes.
- Always check that a loaf is cooked by using a skewer through the middle. The loaf is not cooked until the skewer comes out clean. A part-cooked loaf can be turned over on the baking tray to ensure even cooking.
- All these breads can also be cooked slowly in a frying pan. Cover with a lid and turn several times. Cooking time depends on the temperature and the thickness of the dough.

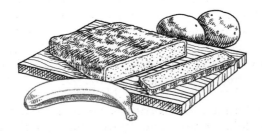

Millet and Banana Bread

MAKES ONE 1 LB LOAF

¼ pint or 150 ml water or milk
1 or 2 eggs
1 large banana
4 oz or 100 g millet flour
4 oz or 100 g rice flour

1 teaspoon bicarbonate of soda
½ teaspoon cream of tartar
salt to taste
2 tablespoons olive oil

- See Rice Bread for method.

Quinnoa Bread

MAKES ONE 1 LB LOAF

4 oz or 100 g quinnoa grain
4 oz or 100 g tofu
4 oz or 100 g gluten-free flour
  mix
1 teaspoon bicarbonate of soda

½ teaspoon cream of tartar
salt to taste
1 oz or 25 g fat or cooking oil
¼ pint or 150 ml water or milk
1 teaspoon sugar

- Soak the quinnoa grain in boiling water for 10 minutes and then drain, discarding the water.
- Leave the grain to soak in 1 pint water overnight. Drain before using and discard this water.
- Liquidise the soaked quinnoa with the tofu to a smooth purée and then beat in the milk. This is best done in a liquidiser.
- Mix all the dry ingredients for the bread together with two tablespoons oil.
- Fold the flour mixture into the purée. Do not overmix and do not leave to stand at this point or you will lose the light structure to the bread dough.
- Place the mixture 1 inch/2.5 cm deep into a shallow 10 inch/25 cm square baking tray lined with non-stick baking parchment.
- Bake in a preheated oven, gas mark 7, 425°F, 220°C, for 35–45 minutes.
- Always check that a loaf is cooked by using a skewer through the middle. The loaf is not cooked until the skewer comes out clean. A part-cooked loaf can be turned over on the baking tray to ensure even cooking.

Apple Bread Rolls

MAKES 12 ROLLS

1 banana
4 oz or 100 g grated apple
¼ pint or 150 ml milk
2 eggs
8 oz or 225 g gluten-free flour mix
1 teaspoon bicarbonate of soda

½ teaspoon cream of tartar
salt to taste
2 oz or 50 g fat or two
 tablespoons olive oil
1 teaspoon sugar

- Beat the banana and apple to a smooth purée with the milk and eggs. This is best done in a liquidiser.
- Mix all the dry ingredients for the rolls together with one tablespoon oil.
- Fold the flour mixture into the purée. Do not overmix and do not leave to stand at this point or you will lose the light structure to the bread dough.
- Grease individual pattie trays or bun trays – put a drop of olive oil in each.
- Spoon the mixture onto the baking trays.
- Bake in a preheated oven, gas mark 7, 425°F, 220°C, for 12 to 15 minutes.
- Remove onto a wire tray to cool.
- Serve hot with Tomato and Apple Soup. See page 69 for recipe.

Variations

CARROT BREAD ROLLS
- Use 4 oz/100 g grated carrot in place of the apple.

MARROW BREAD ROLLS
- Use 4 oz/100 g grated marrow in place of the apple. Serve with marrow and pineapple jam.

Honey Loaf

MAKES ONE 1½ LB LOAF

8 oz or 225 g gluten-free flour
  mix
1 teaspoon bicarbonate of soda
½ teaspoon cream of tartar
salt to taste
3 teaspoons mixed spice

20 oz or 50 g candied peel,
  chopped fine
4 oz or 100 g soft brown sugar
6 oz or 175 g clear honey
¼ pint or 150 ml milk

- Mix all the flours together with the salt and raising agents.
- Add all the remaining ingredients, except milk.
- Add milk and mix in until the mixture will flow slowly.
- Pour the mixture into a greased 2 lb bread tin.
- Bake in a preheated oven, gas mark 6, 400°F, 200°C for 30 minutes and then reduce the temperature to gas mark 2, 300°F, 150°C, until cooked through. Check by using a skewer through the middle. The loaf is not cooked until the skewer comes out clean.
- Allow to stand for 10 minutes before turning out onto a wire tray to cook thoroughly.

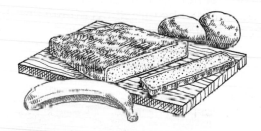

Egg Bread

MAKES ONE 1 LB LOAF

8 oz or 225 g gluten-free flour mix

2 eggs, beaten

¼ pint or 150 ml milk

1 oz or 25 g margarine or 2 tablespoons olive oil

1 teaspoon bicarbonate of soda

½ teaspoon cream of tartar

salt to taste

1 teaspoon sugar

- Beat the milk and egg together.
- Mix all the dry ingredients for the bread together with two tablespoons oil.
- Fold the flour mixture into the beaten egg. Do not overmix and do not leave to stand at this point or you will lose the light structure to the bread dough.
- Place the mixture into a shallow 10 inch/25 cm square baking tray lined with a non-stick baking parchment.
- Bake in a preheated oven, gas mark 7, 425°F, 220°C, for 35–45 minutes.
- Always check that a loaf is cooked by using a skewer through the middle. The loaf is not cooked until the skewer comes out clean. A part-cooked loaf can be turned over on the baking tray to ensure even cooking.
- Turn out onto a wire tray to cool.

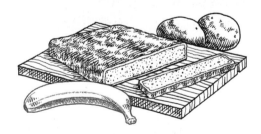

Crispbreads

Millet and Sesame Crispbread

MAKES *12–20* SMALL CRISPBREADS

4 oz or 100 g millet grain	1 tablespoon golden syrup
4 oz or 100 g sesame seed	salt to taste
1 oz or 25 g melted lard	⅛ pint or 75 ml boiling water

- Mix the dry millet and sesame seed together and then grind them into a flour using a grain mill (this does not work so well with a liquidiser).
- Mix in the golden syrup and the melted lard.
- Add a little boiling water until the mixture forms a soft dough.
- Spread over a greased tray and press down well with a spatula to the final thickness of the crispbread (about ⅛ inch or 3 mm). Score into squares.
- Bake in a preheated oven, gas mark 6, 400°F, 200°C, for 8–12 minutes or until golden brown.
- Turn out onto a wire tray to cool and dry.
- Crispbreads can be dried after cooking by placing in a microwave on simmer setting for 10–20 minutes.
- Keep crispbreads in an airtight container.

Corn Crispbread

MAKES 12 SMALL CRISPBREADS

4 oz or 100 g corn meal
4 oz or 100 g ground rice
½ teaspoon bicarbonate of soda
½ teaspoon cream of tartar

1 oz or 25 g melted lard
salt to taste
4 fl oz or 125 ml boiling water

- Mix the flours together with the bicarbonate of soda and cream of tartar.
- Mix in the melted lard.
- Add a little boiling water until the mixture forms soft crumbs that stick together when kneaded. The mixture should feel dry, not wet.
- Take a walnut-sized lump of dough and place it between two sheets of silicone-coated or greaseproof paper. Roll it until it is 2 mm thick. Peel off the paper and place these crispbreads on a greased tray.
- If the paper on top is not easy to remove, cook with the paper in place for the first few minutes, and then peel it away.
- Bake in a preheated oven, gas mark 6, 400°F, 200°C, for 8–12 minutes or until golden brown.
- Turn out onto a wire tray to cool and dry.
- Keep crispbreads in an airtight container.

Sorghum Crispbread

MAKES 12–15 SMALL, VERY HARD, CRISPBREADS

4 oz or 100 g sorghum flour   salt to taste
4 oz or 100 g ground rice   4 fl oz or 125 ml boiling water
2 oz or 50 g margarine or lard

- Mix all the dry ingredients together and rub in the margarine or lard until the mixture is like fine breadcrumbs.
- Add a little boiling water until the mixture forms soft crumbs that stick together when kneaded. The mixture should feel dry, not wet.
- Take a walnut-sized lump of dough and place it between two sheets of silicone-coated or greaseproof paper. Roll it until it is very thin. Peel off the paper and place these crispbreads on a greased tray.
- If the paper is not easy to remove, cook with the top paper in place for the first few minutes, and then peel it away.
- Bake in a preheated oven, gas mark 3, 325°F, 160°C, for 15–20 minutes or until lightly brown.
- Turn out onto a wire tray to cool and dry.

Ground Rice and Buckwheat Crispbread

MAKES 12–15 SMALL CRISPBREADS

4 oz or 100 g ground rice   1 oz or 25 g melted lard
4 oz or 100 g buckwheat flour   1 tablespoon golden syrup
½ teaspoon bicarbonate of soda   salt to taste
½ teaspoon cream of tartar   3 fl oz or 90 ml boiling water

- Mix the dry ingredients together.
- Mix in the golden syrup and the melted lard.
- Add a little boiling water until the mixture forms a soft dough.
- Take a walnut-sized lump of dough and place it between two sheets of silicone-coated or greaseproof paper. Roll it until it is very thin. Peel off the paper and place these crispbreads on a greased tray.

- If the paper is not easy to remove, cook with the top paper in place for the first few minutes, and then peel it away.
- Bake in a preheated oven, gas mark 6, 400°F, 200°C, for 8–12 minutes or until golden brown.
- Turn out onto a wire tray to cool and dry.
- Crispbreads can be dried after cooking by placing in a microwave on simmer setting for 10–15 minutes.
- Keep crispbreads in an airtight container.

Chestnut Crispbread

MAKES 12–15 SMALL CRISPBREADS

4 oz or 100 g sweet chestnut purée (unsweetened)
4 oz or 100 g sunflower seeds

2 oz or 50 g ground rice or sorghum flour
1 oz or 25 g melted lard

- Liquidise the sunflower seeds with the sweet chestnut purée.
- Mix in the melted lard.
- Mix in the flour.
- Take a walnut sized lump of dough and place it between two sheets of silicone-coated or greaseproof paper.
- Roll it until it is 2 mm thick. Peel off the paper and place these crispbreads on a greased tray.
- If the paper on top is not easy to remove, cook with the paper in place for the first few minutes, and then peel away the paper.
- Bake in a preheated oven, gas mark 6, 400°F, 200°C, for 8 to 12 minutes or until golden brown.
- Turn out onto a wire tray to cool and dry.
- Keep crispbreads in an airtight container.

Pancakes

Thin Buckwheat Pancakes

A traditional American recipe

MAKES ABOUT 16 PANCAKES

4 oz or 100 g buckwheat flour *¼ teaspoon salt*
4 oz or 100 g rice flour *1 oz or 25 g margarine*
1 oz or 25 g sugar *2 eggs*
½ teaspoon bicarbonate of soda *½ pint or 280 ml milk or water*
¼ teaspoon cream of tartar

- Mix all the dry ingredients together, then beat in the eggs and fat.
- Gradually add the milk while mixing until the mixture flows slowly. Leave to stand for 30 minutes.
- Beat in a little more milk if this is needed for a thin, dropping consistency.
- Heat a strong frying pan with enough oil to coat the bottom, but no more. The oil should not be hot enough to smoke.
- Pour enough of the batter into the pan to cover the bottom when spread thinly with a spatula.
- Turn when bubbles break on the surface and cook until light brown on both sides. This is not as easy as it sounds because the batter is brown to start with. If you are not sure turn the pancakes several times.
- Serve hot with honey or maple syrup.
- These freeze well but toast them under a grill before using and serve hot. Take care not to overheat when reheating with a microwave.

Sweet Chestnut Pancakes

MAKES 4 LARGE PANCAKES

2 eggs
½ pint or 280 ml milk
4 oz or 100 g sweet chestnut
  purée
4 oz or 100 g gluten-free flour
  mix

pinch salt to taste
½ teaspoon bicarbonate of soda
¼ teaspoon cream of tartar
1 tablespoon olive oil
½ oz or 12 g sugar

- Mix all the dry ingredients.
- Beat in the eggs and the oil and then the milk until the mixture flows slowly.
- Cook on an iron griddle in the traditional way or heat a strong frying pan with enough oil to coat the bottom, but no more. The oil should not be hot enough to smoke.
- Drop spoonfuls of the mixture into the pan. After a few moments turn and flatten the pancakes slightly – they will rise again. Cook until both sides are light-brown.
- Serve hot with butter and jam.
- These freeze well but toast them under a grill before serving.

Variations
- Use sweet chestnut flour in place of sweet chestnut purée (unsweetened).

Scots Pancakes – 1

MAKES ABOUT 12 PANCAKES

1 large banana
2 eggs
9 fl oz or 260 ml milk or water
8 oz or 225 g gluten-free flour
  mix
2 oz or 50 g sugar

pinch salt to taste
½ teaspoon bicarbonate of soda
¼ teaspoon cream of tartar
1 oz or 25 g dripping, lard or
  butter

- Beat the banana to a smooth purée with the milk and egg. This is best done in a liquidiser.
- Mix all the dry ingredients together and beat in the fat, then the liquid mix.
- Cook on an iron griddle in the traditional way or heat a strong frying pan with enough oil to coat the bottom, but no more. The oil should not be hot enough to smoke.
- Drop spoonfuls of the mixture into the pan. After a few moments turn them over.
- Cook until both sides are light-brown.
- Serve hot with butter and jam.

Variations
- Instead of beating in the whole eggs, separate the egg yolk and white. Beat the egg yolks into the mixture and beat the egg whites by themselves until stiff and then fold them into the batter.
- Use 4 oz or 100 g grated apple in place of the banana.

Scots Pancakes – 2

MAKES ABOUT 12 PANCAKES

4 oz or 100 g tofu
2 eggs
½ pint or 280 ml milk
8 oz or 225 g gluten-free flour
  mix

2 oz or 50 g sugar
pinch salt to taste
½ teaspoon bicarbonate of soda
¼ teaspoon cream of tartar
2 tablespoons olive oil

- Beat the chestnut purée or tofu to a smooth purée with the milk and egg. This is best done in a liquidiser.
- Mix all the dry ingredients and the oil
- Beat in the purée.
- Cook on an iron griddle in the traditional way or heat a strong frying pan with enough oil to coat the bottom but no more. The oil should not be hot enough to smoke.
- Drop spoonfuls of the mixture into the pan. After a few moments turn and flatten the pancakes slightly – they will rise again. Cook until both sides are light-brown.
- Serve hot with butter and jam.

Scones

Brown Buckwheat Scones

MAKES 5 SCONES WITH A STRONG FLAVOUR

4 oz or 100 g grated carrot	1 oz or 25 g sugar
1 egg	1 teaspoon bicarbonate of soda
¼ pint or 150 ml milk	½ teaspoon cream of tartar
4 oz or 100 g buckwheat flour	2 oz or 50 g butter or margarine
4 oz or 100 g rice flour	pinch salt to taste

- Beat the carrot to a smooth purée with the milk and egg. This is best done in a liquidiser.
- Mix all the dry ingredients for the scones together with the fat.
- Fold the flour mixture into the purée. Do not overmix and do not leave to stand at this point or you will lose the light structure to the scones.
- Spoon the mixture onto a baking tray lined with non-stick baking parchment or into individual greased pattie tins or a bun tray.
- Bake in a preheated oven, gas mark 7, 425°F, 200°C, for 15–20 minutes until brown.
- Serve hot with butter and jam or with clotted cream and jam.
- Scones freeze well. Serve toasted after freezing.

Variations

SULTANA SCONES
- Add 2 oz or 50 g sultanas or other dried fruit
  ½ teaspoon ground cinnamon

CHEESE SCONES
- Add 2 oz or 50 g grated cheese to the basic dry scone mix.

Other variations
- Use gluten-free flour mix in place of rice flour.
- Use 4 oz or 100 g prunes in place of the carrot.

117

Potato Scones

MAKES 12 SCONES

¼ pint or 150 ml milk
2 eggs, beaten
4 oz or 100 g cooked potato
4 oz or 100 g gluten-free flour
 mix
1 teaspoon bicarbonate of soda

½ teaspoon cream of tartar
2 oz or 50 g butter, margarine
 or two tablespoons olive oil
pinch salt to taste
1 oz or 25 g sugar

- Beat the cooked potato to a smooth purée with the milk and egg. This is best done in a liquidiser.
- Mix all the dry ingredients for the scones together with the fat.
- Fold the flour mixture into the purée. Do not overmix and do not leave to stand at this point or you will lose the light structure to the scones.
- Spoon the mixture onto a greased baking tray or use greased individual pattie tins or a bun tray.
- Bake in a preheated oven, gas mark 7, 425°F, 200°C, for 15–20 minutes until brown.

Cakes and buns

Cornflour and potato flour make a very light and white cake mixture but they tend to produce a very dry sponge cake. Rice flour produces a grey cake, but still with a tendency to dryness. These flours cannot support fruit on their own in a fruit cake and the fruit tends to sink as the cake is cooked.

Apple and banana will add moisture to sponge cakes, but both give the cake a strong flavour. They give a fruit cake the strength to support the fruit. Sweet chestnut flour and ground almonds both give a sponge cake a much better texture and can support the fruit in a fruit cake. Sorghum flour will also make excellent fruit cakes.

Carob flour has a strong flavour but burns easily when cooked and should not be used for any recipe cooked at a high temperature.

Chestnut purée has an excellent mild flavour and can be used in both sponge cakes and fruit cakes. To make a chestnut purée, obtain fresh sweet chestnuts, usually in most supermarkets at Christmas. Blanch them by cutting in half and then boiling for 3 minutes, after which the skins are easily removed. They can be converted to a purée in a food processor and stored in the freezer until needed. Chestnut purée is also available in tins in most supermarkets. Use the unsweetened purée for making cakes. Tofu or prunes can be used in the same way to keep cakes moist.

Rich, flour-less sponges are idea for special occasion cakes. These often sink in the middle when cooking, but if this is a problem, try cooking the sponge in a ring-shaped tin.

The flours in the following recipes produce grey or darker-coloured sponge cakes but a tiny pinch of saffron will give a cake a rich yellow colour.

Cooking times can vary a lot depending on variation in size of the eggs and on the position of the cake in the oven. Check to see if a cake is cooked by inserting a skewer or a thin-bladed knife through the middle to the base of the cake. The cake is not cooked until the skewer comes out clean, not sticky. If the top of the cake is cooking too quickly, cover the baking tin with a metal or foil lid for the remainder of the cooking period.

Ann's Sticky Chocolate Cake

MAKES AN 8 INCH/20 CM CAKE

4 eggs
4 oz or 100 g butter
4 oz or 100 g caster sugar
4 oz or 100 g plain chocolate
(**not** cooking chocolate)

3 oz or 75 g ground almonds
1 oz or 25 g potato flour

- Separate the eggs.
- Put the chocolate in the mixing bowl over a pan of simmering water to melt, or place in the microwave on medium for 1 minute.
- Whisk in the butter and sugar, egg yolks and ground almonds.
- Beat the egg whites separately until stiff and then fold into the mixture together with the potato flour.
- Put the mixture into a shallow, round 8 inch/20 cm sponge tin lined with non-stick baking parchment.
- Bake in a preheated oven, gas mark 3, 325°F, 160°C, for about 55 minutes to 1¼ hours.
- Let the cake cool in the tin before turning out.
- This cake will often sink slightly in the middle.
- Serve with the hollow filled with whipped cream.

Eileen's Chocolate Hazelnut Gateau

MAKES AN 8 INCH/20 CM CAKE

4 eggs
4 oz or 100 g butter
4 oz or 100 g caster sugar
4 oz or 100 g ground hazelnuts
4 oz or 100 g plain chocolate
(**not** cooking chocolate)

2 teaspoons instant coffee,
dissolved in 1 tablespoon
boiling water
2 teaspoons rum (either white
or dark)

- Separate the eggs
- Put the chocolate in the mixing bowl over a pan of simmering water to melt or place in the microwave on medium for 1 minute.
- Whisk in the butter and sugar, egg yolks, ground hazelnuts, coffee powder and rum.
- Beat the egg whites separately until stiff and then fold into the mixture.
- Put the mixture into an 8 inch/20 cm sponge tin lined with non-stick baking parchment.
- Bake in a preheated oven, gas mark 1, 275°F, 140°C, for about 1¼–1½ hours.
- Let the cake cool in the tin before turning out.
- This cake will often sink slightly in the middle.
- Serve with the hollow filled with whipped cream.

Variations
- Flavour with brandy or orange juice instead of rum.
- Use ground almonds in place of ground hazelnuts.

Boiled Fruit Cake

This recipe makes an excellent cutting cake.

MAKES A 1½ LB CAKE IN AN 8 INCH/20 CM TIN

1 large banana	¼ pint or 150 ml hot water
4 oz or 100 g grated carrot	8 oz or 225 g gluten-free flour
2 eggs	mix
4 oz or 100 g margarine, hard	½ teaspoon bicarbonate of soda
4 oz or 100 g sugar	¼ teaspoon cream of tartar
8 oz or 225 g mixed dried fruit	1 teaspoon mixed spice
several glacé cherries	

- Put the margarine, sugar, mixed fruit and hot water in a large pan and stir over low heat until the fat has melted and the sugar dissolved.
- Simmer gently for 5–10 minutes before cooling until lukewarm
- Beat the banana and carrot to a smooth purée with the egg. This is best done in a liquidiser.
- Beat the purée into the cooled fruit mixture.
- Mix the flours together with the bicarbonate of soda, cream of tartar and mixed spice.
- Fold the flour mixture in quickly to the cooled fruit mixture and pour the mixture immediately into a deep 8 inch/20 cm cake or 2 lb loaf tin lined with a layer of non-stick baking parchment.
- Bake in a preheated oven, gas mark 4, 350°F, 180°C for 1¼–1½ hours.
- Cool in tin before turning out and removing parchment.

Variations
- Use 4 oz or 100 g unsweetened tinned chestnut purée or 4 oz/100 g prunes or 4 oz/100 g tofu in place of the banana.

Banana Sponge Cake

This makes a light, moist sponge cake with a strong banana flavour.

MAKES A 7 INCH/18 CM SPONGE

½ large banana	2 oz or 50 g sugar
1 large egg	3 oz or 75 g gluten-free flour mix
¾ oz or 20 g butter or soft margarine	½ teaspoon bicarbonate of soda
	¼ teaspoon cream of tartar

- Beat the banana to a smooth purée with the egg. This is best done in a liquidiser.
- Cream the butter and sugar.
- In a separate bowl, sieve together the flours, bicarbonate of soda, cream of tartar.
- Beat the egg and banana gradually into the butter and sugar. This is better done by hand than in a mixer.
- Fold the flour into the egg mixture and immediately place the mixture in a greased, 7 inch/18 cm sponge tin lined with non-stick baking parchment.
- Bake in a preheated oven, gas mark 3, 325°F, 160°C, for 20–25 minutes, when the top should be golden brown and the sides shrinking away from the tin.
- Stand for 10 minutes before turning out onto a wire tray to cool.

Variations
- Flavour with 1 teaspoon cocoa powder, 1 drop vanilla essence or grated zest of one lemon added to the sugar.
- Use sorghum flour to make a dark sponge.

BIRTHDAY CAKE
- Make one 8 inch/20 cm vanilla sponge cake and one 8 inch/ 20 cm chocolate sponge cake
- Sandwich the two cakes together with a layer of butter-cream icing.
- Spread the top of the cake with white icing or butter-cream icing.

CAROB SPONGE CAKE
- Replace half the gluten-free flour with carob flour.

Sweet Chestnut Sponge Cake

This makes a light, moist sponge cake with a superb flavour. The chestnut gives it a dark colour, so cover it with a chocolate butter-cream icing or melted chocolate.

MAKES A 7 INCH/18 CM SPONGE

3 oz or 75 g unsweetened, tinned chestnut purée
1 large egg
1½ oz or 30 g butter or soft margarine

2 oz or 50 g sugar
2 oz or 50 g cornflour
1 oz or 25 g potato flour
½ teaspoon bicarbonate of soda
¼ teaspoon cream of tartar

- Beat the chestnut purée to a smooth purée with the egg. This is best done in a liquidiser.
- Cream the butter and sugar.
- In a separate bowl sieve together the flours, bicarbonate of soda and cream of tartar.
- Beat the egg and chestnut purée gradually into the butter and sugar. This is better done by hand than in a mixer.
- Fold the flour into the egg mixture and immediately place the mixture in a greased, 7 inch/18 cm sponge tin lined with non-stick baking parchment.
- Bake in a preheated oven, gas mark 3, 325°F, 160°C, for 20–25 minutes when the top should be golden brown and the sides shrinking away from the tin.
- Stand for 10 minutes before turning out onto a wire tray to cool.

Variations
- Flavour with 1 teaspoon cocoa powder, 1 drop vanilla essence or grated zest of one lemon added to the sugar.

BIRTHDAY CAKE
- Make one 8 inch/20 cm vanilla sponge cake and one 8 inch/ 20 cm chocolate sponge cake.
- Sandwich the two cakes together with a layer of chocolate butter-cream icing.
- Spread the top of the cake with melted chocolate.

Almond Sponge Cake

MAKES AN 8 INCH/20 CM SPONGE

4 oz or 100 g butter or soft
  margarine
7 oz or 200 g sugar

4 large eggs
7 oz or 200 g ground almonds
1 teaspoon almond essence

- Beat the sugar and eggs together until they double in volume.
- Mix in the butter and then the ground almonds and almond essence.
- Place the mixture in greased 8 inch/20 cm sponge tin lined with non-stick baking parchment.
- Bake in a preheated oven, gas mark 4, 350°F, 180°C, for 30–45 minutes when the top should be golden brown and the sides shrinking away from the tin.
- Stand for 10 minutes before turning out onto a wire tray to cool.
- When cold cover with a white icing and decorate with angelica strips and glacé cherries.

Bataclan Almond Sponge Cake

A light and reliable sponge cake, based on a traditional French recipe.

MAKES AN 8 INCH/20 CM CAKE

4 oz or 100 g ground almonds
5 oz or 125 g sugar
2 oz or 50 g gluten-free flour
* mix*

4 large eggs
1 tablespoon or 40 ml rum
1 drop vanilla essence

- Beat the eggs one at a time into the almonds. This is best done with a food processor.
- Mix in the sugar, vanilla essence and rum.
- Then gradually add the flour, mixing well to form a smooth paste.
- Place the mixture in a greased and lined 8 inch/20 cm sponge tin.
- Bake in a preheated oven, gas mark 4, 350°F, 180°C, for 30–45 minutes.
- Stand for 10 minutes before turning out onto a wire tray.
- When cold cover with a white vanilla icing.

Variations
- Can be flavoured with lemon, chocolate or coffee added to the sugar, instead of the vanilla.

Dundee Cake

MAKES ONE 2 LB CAKE

1 large banana
4 oz or 100 g grated carrot
3 fl oz or 90 ml milk
3 large eggs
5 oz or 150 g butter or margarine
5 oz or 150 g sugar
8 oz or 225 g gluten-free flour
  mix
1 teaspoon bicarbonate of soda
½ teaspoon cream of tartar

6 oz or 175 g currants
6 oz or 175 g sultanas
2 oz or 50 g glacé cherries
2 oz or 50 g finely chopped peel
1 oz or 25 g ground almonds
grated rind one small orange
  and one small lemon
2 oz or 50 g whole blanched
  almonds

- Beat the banana and carrot to a smooth purée with the milk and egg. This is best done in a liquidiser.
- Beat together the butter and sugar.
- Beat the purée gradually into the creamed mixture.
- In a separate bowl sieve together the flours and bicarbonate of soda, cream of tartar and mix before adding the ground almonds.
- In a separate bowl mix together the currants, sultanas, mixed peel, grated rind and glacé cherries.
- Fold the flour gently into the creamed mixture.
- Gently fold the fruit into the cake mixture.
- Immediately spoon the mixture gently into a deep 8 inch/20 cm cake tin lined with non-stick baking parchment.
- Smooth the top and place the blanched almonds on top to decorate. Do not push these into the mixture.
- Bake in a preheated oven, gas mark 3, 325°F, 160°C, for 1½–2 hours, or gas mark 2 for 2–2½ hours.
- Let the cake cool before turning it out onto a wire tray.
- Store in an airtight tin. This cake keeps well.

Variations
- Use chopped dates or dried apricots in place of the cherries.
- Use 4 oz/100 g unsweetened tinned chestnut purée or 4 oz/100 g tofu or 4 oz/100 g prunes in place of the banana.

Liqueur Cake

MAKES ONE RICH YELLOW 1 LB CAKE

4 oz or 100 g ground almonds
4 oz or 100 g sugar
2 eggs
6 egg yolks
4 oz or 100 g gluten-free flour
  mix

one small glass liqueur
  (Benedictine, cherry brandy,
  apricot brandy, etc)
apricot jam

- Keep the mixture cool.
- Beat together the ground almonds and sugar.
- Then beat in the egg yolks one at a time.
- Then beat in the whole eggs one at a time.
- Mix in one tablespoon liqueur.
- In a separate bowl sieve together the flours.
- Fold the flours gently into the mixture a little at a time.
- Spoon the mixture gently into an 8 inch/20 cm cake tin lined with non-stick baking parchment.
- Bake in a preheated oven, gas mark 4, 350°F, 180°C, for 45 minutes–1 hour.
- Stand for 10 minutes before turning out onto a wire tray to cool.
- Pour the remaining liqueur on top of the cake and then cover with apricot jam.
- Use the egg white to make meringues.

Mincemeat Cake

MAKES ONE 2 LB CAKE

1 large banana
4 oz or 100 g grated carrot
3 fl oz or 90 ml milk
3 large eggs
5 oz or 150 g butter or margarine
5 oz or 150 g soft brown sugar
8 oz or 225 g gluten-free flour
  mix
1 teaspoon bicarbonate of soda

½ teaspoon cream of tartar
1 lb or 450 g mincemeat, gluten
  free. See page 136 for recipe.
3 oz or 75 g mixed dried fruit
2 oz or 50 g finely chopped
  walnuts
1 oz or 25 g ground almonds
grated rind one small orange
  and one small lemon

- Beat the banana and carrot to a smooth purée with the milk and egg. This is best done in a liquidiser.
- Beat together the butter and sugar.
- Beat the purée gradually into the creamed mixture.
- In a separate bowl sieve together the flours and bicarbonate of soda, cream of tartar and mix before adding the ground almonds.
- In a separate bowl mix together the mincemeat, mixed fruit and chopped walnuts and grated rind.
- Fold the flour gently into the creamed mixture.
- Gently fold the fruit in the cake mixture.
- Immediately spoon the mixture gently into an 8 inch/20 cm cake tin lined with non-stick baking parchment.
- Bake in a preheated oven, gas mark 3, 325°F, 160°C, for 1½–2 hours.
- Let the cake cool before turning it out onto a wire tray.
- Store in an airtight container. This cake keeps well.

Variations
- Use chopped dates or dried apricots in place of the cherries.
- Use 4 oz/100 g grated apple in place of the banana.

White Icing

FOR AN 8 INCH/20 CM CAKE

5 oz or 150 g sifted icing sugar   1 tablespoon water

- Stir the sifted icing sugar in a bowl and add the water very gradually, drop by drop, until a soft paste forms.
- Spread the icing paste gently on top of the cake.

Butter-cream Icing

FOR A SINGLE 8 INCH/20 CM CAKE

2–3 oz or 50–75 g icing sugar   2 oz or 50 g butter
flavouring as required

- Cream the butter by beating it until it is light and fluffy, then beat in the icing sugar until the desired texture and sweetness is reached.
- Beat in the flavouring.
- Butter-cream icing can be kept for up to three weeks in the refrigerator.

Flavourings
- 1 oz or 25 g melted plain chocolate
     or
- 1 teaspoon cocoa powder
     or
- 1 teaspoon instant coffee powder
     or
- 1 tablespoon orange juice
     or
- 1 drop vanilla essence

Gingerbread

MAKES ONE 1 LB GINGERBREAD

2 eggs
1 large banana
4 oz or 100 g grated carrot
4 oz or 100g sultanas (optional)
4 oz or 100 g margarine or
  butter
6 oz or 175 g black treacle
2 oz or 50 g golden syrup

2 oz or 50 g brown sugar
8 oz or 225 g gluten-free flour
  mix
1 teaspoon bicarbonate of soda
½ teaspoon cream of tartar
1 rounded teaspoon mixed spice
2 level teaspoons ground ginger

- In a large saucepan melt together the margarine, treacle, syrup and sugar over a gentle heat and allow to cool.
- Beat the banana and carrot to a smooth purée with the egg. This is best done in a liquidiser. You can also add 4 oz/100 g sultanas and liquidise them as well.
- Beat the purée into the cooled mixture.
- In a separate bowl, mix all the flours together with the raising agents and spices.
- Fold the flour gently into the cooled mixture and immediately pour the mixture into a greased 2 lb bread tin lined with non-stick baking parchment.
- Bake in a preheated oven, gas mark 2, 300°F, 150°C, for 1¼–2 hours.
- Stand for 10 minutes before turning out onto a wire tray to cool.

Sweet Chestnut Gingercake

MAKES ONE ½ LB CAKE

1 egg
3 oz or 75 g unsweetened, tinned
  chestnut purée
2 oz or 50 g margarine or butter
3 oz or 75 g black treacle
1 oz or 25 g golden syrup
1 oz or 25 g brown sugar

4 oz or 100 g gluten-free flour
  mix
½ teaspoon bicarbonate of soda
¼ teaspoon cream of tartar
1 level teaspoon mixed spice
1 level teaspoon ground ginger

- In a large saucepan, melt together the margarine, treacle, syrup and sugar over a gentle heat and allow to cool.
- Beat the chestnut purée to a smooth purée with the egg. This is best done in a liquidiser.
- Beat the purée into the cooled mixture.
- In a separate bowl mix all the flours, together with the raising agents and spices.
- Fold the flour gently into the cooled mixture and immediately pour the mixture into a greased 7 inch/18 cm sponge tin lined with non-stick baking parchment.
- Bake in a preheated oven, gas mark 2, 300°F, 150°C, for 35–45 minutes.
- Stand for 10 minutes before turning out onto a wire tray to cool.

Margaret's Swiss Roll

MAKES ONE SWISS ROLL

3 large eggs
4 oz or 100 g caster sugar
1 oz or 25 g cocoa powder

6 oz or 175 g plain chocolate
 (not cooking chocolate)
½ pint or 280 ml double cream

- Separate the egg yolks and whites.
- Whip the egg yolks until they thicken.
- Beat in the sugar and beat until thick again.
- Mix in the cocoa well.
- Whip the egg whites separately until stiff.
- Fold the whites gently into the yolk and cocoa mixture.
- Pour the mixture into swiss roll tin lined with non-stick baking parchment.
- Bake at gas mark 3, 325°F, 160°C, for 20 minutes or until the mixture is set.
- Allow to cool before turning out onto a sheet lightly dusted with caster sugar.
- Melt the chocolate bar over a gentle heat. Allow it to cool slightly and then pour over the sponge base.
- Whip the double cream until thick.
- Spread the cream evenly over chocolate-coated base.
- Roll with care, dust with icing sugar and serve.

Sweet Potato Cake

*8 oz or 225 g flesh of sweet
  potato, precooked
6 oz or 175 g sugar
6 oz or 175 g gluten-free flour
4 oz or 100 g chopped almonds
2 oz or 50 g coconut flour or
  desiccated coconut*

*4 fl oz or 125 ml olive oil
1 teaspoon ground cinnamon
½ teaspoon ground nutmeg
½ teaspoon bicarbonate of soda
¼ teaspoon cream of tartar
2 egg whites*

- Precook the sweet potato by baking or boiling until soft. Then drain and peel.
- Beat in all the ingredients except for the egg white. This is best done in a food processor.
- Beat the egg white separately until stiff.
- Fold the egg white into the cake mixture.
- Place the mixture into a deep 8 inch/20 cm cake tin or 2 lb loaf tin lined with non-stick baking parchment.
- Bake in a preheated oven, gas mark 4, 350°F, 180°C for 1¼–1½ hours.
- Cool in tin before turning out and removing parchment.

Pumpkin and Apricot Cake

1 small young pumpkin or squash
 – about the size of a large
 grapefruit
4 dried apricots, chopped finely
1 tablespoon orange peel
2 tablespoons raisins or sultanas
2 oz or 50 g sugar
2 tablespoons olive oil
1 egg

1 teaspoon ground ginger
2 tablespoons dark fruit jelly –
 blueberry or blackberry
⅓ teaspoon ground nutmeg
4 oz or 100 g gluten-free flour
 mix
½ teaspoon bicarbonate of soda
½ teaspoon cream of tartar

- Peel the pumpkin and remove the seeds and pulp. Chop the flesh.
- Beat the pumpkin to a purée with the egg, sugar and oil.
- Beat in all the remaining ingredients.
- Put the mixture into a deep 8 inch/20 cm cake tin lined with non-stick baking parchment.
- Bake in a preheated oven, gas mark 4, 350°F, 180°C for 1¼–1½ hours.

Christmas and party

Mincemeat

Do not use packet suet as this may have been rolled in flour, unless it is on the gluten-free food list.

MAKES 2 LB MINCEMEAT

1 lemon
4 oz or 100 g sultanas
4 oz or 100 g raisins
4 oz or 100 g currants
8 oz or 225 g apples, with cores
  removed
4 oz or 100 g suet
1 oz or 25 g candied peel, mixed

4 oz or 100 g caster sugar
¼ teaspoon mixed spice
¼ teaspoon ground ginger
¼ teaspoon ground nutmeg
¼ teaspoon ground cinnamon
¼ teaspoon ground mace
⅛ pint or 75 ml brandy

- Chop the lemon, peel and all, and cook in a little water until soft. Then chop finely in a food processor.
- Chop all the remaining fruit and suet in small quantities in a food processor quite finely.
- Mix all the chopped fruit together with the lemon, suet and spices and sugar.
- Mix in the brandy, cover the bowl and leave to stand for 24 hours. Mix again before pressing into jars.
- Keep for at least two weeks before using.

Christmas Cake
Heather's recipe

MAKES ONE 5 LB CAKE

2 lb or 900 g mixed dried fruit
4 oz or 100 g glacé cherries
8 fl oz or 230 ml rum (dark)
5 eggs, separated
1 large banana

6 oz or 175 g gluten-free flour
  mix
8 oz or 225 g butter
8 oz or 225 g soft brown sugar
¼ pint or 150 ml clear honey

- Soak the dried fruit and cherries in rum for 24 hours.
- Separate the eggs.
- Beat the banana to a smooth purée with the egg yolks. This is best done in a liquidiser.
- Mix the flours together.
- Cream the butter and sugar together.
- Add the purée to the butter and sugar, beating in with spoonfuls of flour added gradually. Then fold in the remaining flour.
- Stir in the dried fruit and rum.
- Stir in the honey.
- Beat the egg whites stiff and then fold in.
- Place the mixture in a deep 9 inch/23 cm cake tin lined with non-stick baking parchment.
- Bake in a preheated oven, gas mark 3, 325°F, 160°C, for 2–2½ hours – check after 1 hour and cover the top if this is browning too rapidly.

Variations
- Use 4 oz/100 g unsweetened tinned chestnut purée or 4 oz/100 g tofu in place of the banana.

Christmas Pudding

MAKES TWO 2 LB PUDDINGS

*4 oz or 100 g unsweetened,
tinned chestnut purée*
4 eggs
¼ pint or 150 ml milk
2 oz or 50 g grated apple
2 oz or 50 g rice flour
*8 oz or 225 g gluten-free
breadcrumbs*
*8 oz or 225 g fresh suet, grated
in processor*
2 oz or 50 g ground almonds
8 oz or 225 g sugar

8 oz or 225 g currants
8 oz or 225 g sultanas
8 oz or 225 g raisins
4 oz or 100 g mixed peel
2 oz or 50 g glacé cherries
2 oz or 50 g black treacle
1 lemon, grated and squeezed
1 wineglass brandy
¼ teaspoon salt
1 teaspoon ground nutmeg
1 teaspoon ground cinnamon

- Beat the chestnut and apple to a smooth purée with the milk and egg. This is best done in a liquidiser.
- Sift the flours into a large mixing bowl and mix in the purée. Gradually mix in all the remaining ingredients, stirring well.
- Place the mixture in well-greased pudding basins. They should not be overful. Cover with greaseproof paper and then aluminium foil tied tightly round the top of the bowl.
- A one-pint basin should be steamed for 4 hours. A two-pint basin should be steamed for 6 hours.
- If a pressure cooker is available steam for 30 minutes without pressure and then for 3 hours under 15 lb (high) pressure.
- **Always check water levels when steaming for several hours.**
- Steam for 2–3 hours to reheat before serving.

Variations
- Use a large banana in place of the chestnut
- Use 100 ml olive oil in place of suet.

Mince Pies

MAKES 6 MINCE PIES

8 oz or 225 g prepared shortcrust   8 oz or 225 g mincemeat,
potato pastry. See page 165   gluten-free
for ingredients.

- Roll out the pastry between two sheets of non-stick silicone-coated parchment.
- Cut six larger pastry circles for the base and six smaller for the tops.
- Use the parchment to help transfer the pastry bases to a greased bun tray.
- Fill each pastry base with mincemeat.
- Brush round the edge of each base with milk or egg before placing the pastry top over the base. It is easiest to position the soft pastry by using the parchment and then peeling the parchment away.
- Bake in a preheated oven, gas mark 5, 375°F, 190°C, for 20–25 minutes or until the tops are brown.

Chocolate Fondue

SERVES 6

8 oz or 225 g plain chocolate   cubes of fresh fruit, marsh
(not cooking chocolate)   mallow and gluten-free
5 fl oz or 150 ml double cream   sponge cake

- Grate the chocolate into the fondue pan with the cream and stir continuously until the chocolate melts and the fondue is ready to serve. Do not heat beyond this point, the cream should never get anywhere near boiling point.
- Each person dips their selection into the fondue with a long fork and eats it while still hot.

Variations
- Add 1 teaspoon instant coffee powder to the fondue.
- For adults add 2 tablespoons/30 ml Kirsch, Tia Maria or Creme Cacao to the hot fondue.

Biscuits

Rice Biscuits

MAKES 20

8 oz or 225 g rice flour
4 oz or 100 g caster sugar
4 oz or 100 g butter or margarine

1 egg
flavouring

- Beat the butter into a cream.
- Beat the egg.
- Stir the flour and sugar into the butter.
- Stir the egg into the mixture and mix well.
- Roll small balls of the mixture and then flatten these onto a greased baking tray.
- Bake in a preheated oven, gas mark 4, 350°F, 180°C, for 12–18 minutes until brown.
- Turn out onto a wire tray to cool and dry.
- Store in an airtight container.

Flavourings
- 1 oz or 25 g cocoa powder
    or
- 1 teaspoon instant coffee powder
    or
- 1 tablespoon orange juice
    or
- 2 drops of vanilla essence

Almond Biscuits

MAKES 48 SMALL BISCUITS

4 oz or 100 g sugar
4 oz or 100 g butter
4 oz or 100 g ground almonds
4 oz or 100 g gluten-free flour
  mix

1 egg
2 oz or 50 g chopped almonds

- Cream the butter and sugar together, then work in the ground almonds and flour.
- Separate the egg yolk and white and keep a little of the white.
- Beat the rest of the egg and add a little at a time to the mixture, working it in until a firm dough is produced.
- Roll our ⅛ inch/3 mm thick and cut into rounds or shapes.
- Brush the dough with white of egg and decorate with chopped almonds.
- Bake in a preheated oven, gas mark 4, 350°F, 180°C, for 10–12 minutes or until they are golden brown.
- Cook on a wire tray and store in an airtight container.

Ginger Snaps

MAKES 24

6 oz or 175 gluten-free flour mix
½ teaspoon bicarbonate of soda
½ teaspoon cream of tartar
2 teaspoons ground ginger

4 oz or 100 g sugar
2 oz or 50 g lard
1½ oz or 40 g golden syrup
1 egg

- Sift all the dry ingredients together.
- Melt the lard and the syrup together and allow these to cool slightly before adding to the dry mixture.
- Beat the egg before adding to the mixture, which now should form a firm dough.
- Shape the dough into walnut-sized balls and place them well apart on a greased tray.
- Bake in a preheated oven, gas mark 5, 375°F, 190°C, for 15–20 minutes or until they are brown.

Variations
- For gingerbread men use treacle in place of syrup and reduce the raising agent to just ½ teaspoon bicarbonate of soda.
- Roll out the dough until less than ¼ inch/5 mm thick and then cut to shape.

Ginger Biscuits

Makes 20

7 oz or 200 g gluten-free flour mix *1 egg*
1 oz or 25 g ground almonds *4 oz or 100 g butter or*
4 oz or 100 g sugar   *margarine*
¼ oz or 5 g ground ginger *a little milk if needed*

- Mix the dry ingredients together first and then rub in the butter or margarine.
- Mix in the egg. If the mixture is too dry add a little milk until it just sticks together in lumps.
- Roll into little balls and then flatten these onto a greased baking tray.
- Bake in a preheated oven, gas mark 3, 325°F, 160°C, for 10–15 minutes until golden brown.
- Turn out onto a wire tray to cool and dry.
- Store in an airtight container.

French Ginger Sponge Biscuits

MAKES 20

4 eggs
4 oz or 100 g sugar

¼ oz or 5 g ground ginger
4 oz or 100 g gluten-free flour mix

- Separate the eggs.
- Mix the egg yolks with the sugar and ginger to form a smooth paste.
- Mix in the flours.
- Beat the egg whites until stiff and then fold this gently into the mixture.
- Cover a baking tray with non-stick baking parchment or use greased bun trays.
- Spoon the mixture onto the paper, or pipe to form small sticks.
- Dust with caster sugar.
- Bake in a preheated oven, gas mark 4, 350°F, 180°C, for 8–10 minutes.
- Turn out onto a wire tray to cool and dry.

French Lemon Sponge Biscuits

MAKES 20

3 eggs
4 oz or 100 g sugar
2 oz or 50 g rice flour

1 oz or 25 g potato flour
1 oz or 25 g ground almonds
1 lemon

- Separate the eggs.
- Mix the egg yolks with the sugar and beat until it forms a stiff paste.
- Mix in the ground almonds, the rice flour and potato flour and the grated rind of the lemon.
- Beat the egg whites until stiff and then fold this gently into the mixture.
- Cover a baking tray with greaseproof or non-stick baking parchment.
- Spoon the mixture onto the paper.
- Dust with caster sugar.

- Bake in a preheated oven, gas mark 3, 325°F, 160°C, for 8–10 minutes.
- Turn out onto a wire tray and return to the oven, gas mark 1, for 1 hour.

Macaroons

MAKES 12

2 egg whites
4 oz or 100 g almonds
7 oz or 200 g caster sugar
1 oz or 25 g sugar

½ oz or 10 g rice flour
1 teaspoon almond essence
blanched almonds to decorate

- Beat the egg whites until thick and stiff and then fold in the remaining ingredients.
- Pipe or spoon onto a greased tray or non-stick baking parchment leaving room to spread.
- Do not use rice paper.
- Place an almond in the middle of each biscuit to decorate it.
- Bake in a preheated oven, gas mark 4, 350°F, 180°C, for 10–15 minutes until light brown.

Coconut Macaroons

MAKES 25

8 oz or 225 g desiccated coconut
6 rounded tablespoons puffed rice cereal

400 g tin condensed milk

- Mix all ingredients together.
- Line a baking tray with non-stick baking parchment and spoon the mixture to form 25 biscuits.
- Bake at gas mark 4, 350°F, 180°C, for 25–30 minutes or until lightly browned.
- Cool on the baking sheet. When cold, lift off the paper and store in an airtight container.

Shortbread

MAKES ONE ROUND

6 oz or 175 g gluten-free flour   4 oz or 100 g hard margarine
  mix   or butter
2 oz or 50 g sugar

- Mix all the dry ingredients together. Then rub in the butter until a fine mixture or soft dough is produced – this will depend on the type of butter or margarine used.
- Press well into a greased tray to the final thickness required for the biscuits. It is much easier to make one large shortbread and score it before cooking than to make separate biscuits.
- Bake in a preheated oven, gas mark 2, 300°F, 150°C, for 30–40 minutes until light brown.

Variations

GINGER SHORTBREAD
- Add ½ oz/12 g ground ginger to the dry ingredients.

CINNAMON SHORTBREAD
- Add ¼ oz/6 g ground cinnamon to the dry ingredients.

Chocolate Biscuits

MAKES 20

1 oz or 25 g cocoa powder   3 oz or 75 g sugar
1 oz or 25 g ground almonds   3 oz or 75 g hard margarine or
5 oz or 150 g gluten-free flour   butter
  mix   1 egg

- Mix all the dry ingredients together.
- Beat the egg before adding it to the dry ingredients with the butter and mix together until a soft dough is produced that sticks into a large ball.
- Break the dough into walnut-sized pieces and place on a greased tray or non-stick baking parchment

- Flatten each lump with the back of a fork dipped in cold water.
- Bake in a preheated oven, gas mark 4, 350°F, 180°C, for 12–15 minutes.
- Cool on a wire tray.

Variations
- Add chopped nuts or crystallised ginger.

Peanut Biscuits

MAKES 36

4 oz or 100 g brown sugar
2 oz or 50 g sugar
3 oz or 75 g hard margarine
2 oz or 50 g crunchy peanut
  butter
1 egg
3 oz or 75 g gluten-free flour mix

1 oz or 25 g ground almonds
2 oz or 50 g corn meal or polenta
½ teaspoon bicarbonate of soda
¼ teaspoon cream of tartar
2 oz or 50 g chopped peanuts
½ teaspoon ground cinnamon

- Cream together the sugar, butter and peanut butter and then beat in the egg.
- Mix all the dry ingredients together with the chopped peanuts.
- Fold the mixed dry ingredients into the butter mixture.
- Break the dough into walnut-sized pieces and place on a greased tray or baking parchment. Flatten each lump with the back of a fork dipped in cold water.
- Bake in a preheated oven, gas mark 4, 350°F, 180°C, for 12–15 minutes or until the edges are light brown.
- Cool on a wire tray.

Variations
- Add chopped nuts or crystallised ginger.

Chocolate Fruit Slice

MAKES 1¼ LB

6 oz or 175 g plain chocolate
 (not cooking chocolate)
6 oz or 175 g mixed dried fruit
2 oz or 50 g glacé cherries

2 oz or 50 g shredded coconut
2 oz or 50 g caster sugar
1 oz or 25 g butter, melted
1 egg, beaten

- Line a shallow 8 × 6 inch/20 × 15 cm tin with foil.
- Melt the chocolate and spread it evenly in the base of the tin. Leave this to cool in the fridge until set.
- Mix all the other ingredients together and spread over the solid chocolate in the tin.
- Bake in a preheated oven, gas mark 4, 350°F, 180°C, for 20–25 minutes until the top is golden brown.
- When the tin is cool, place in the fridge for at least 1 hour until cold.
- When cold, cut into fingers and turn out of the tin.

Date and Apple Slice

MAKES 2 LB

1 lb or 450 g eating apples,
 chopped
3 oz or 75 g mixed chopped nuts
4 oz or 100 g chopped dates
4 oz or 100 g lentil flour or gram
 flour

4 oz or 100 g caster sugar
1 oz or 25 g melted butter
1 tablespoon honey
1 egg, beaten
salt to taste

- Line a shallow 11 × 8 inch/28 × 20 cm tin with foil.
- Mix all the ingredients together and spread over the foil in the tin.
- Bake in a preheated oven, gas mark 4, 350°F, 180°C, for 20–30 minutes until the top is golden brown.
- When cold, cut into fingers and turn out of the tin.

Apricot and Sesame Slice

MAKES 1 LB

2 oz or 50 g butter or margarine
2 oz or 50 g golden syrup
2 oz or 50 g demerara sugar
2 oz or 50 g shredded coconut
4 oz or 100 g flaked rice
2 oz or 50 g chopped dried
  apricots

1 oz or 25 g untoasted sesame
  seeds
2 oz or 50 g plain chocolate
  (not cooking chocolate)
½ teaspoon ground cinnamon
salt to taste

- Line a shallow 11 × 8 inch/28 × 20 cm tin with foil.
- Melt the butter and syrup together over a low heat.
- Chill the chocolate and then crush it into chips.
- Mix all the other ingredients together and then mix in the butter and syrup.
- Mix the chocolate chips in last.
- Spread the mixture over the foil in the tin and press down well.
- Bake in a preheated oven, gas mark 2, 300°F, 150°C, for 30–35 minutes.
- When cold, cut into fingers and turn out of the tin.

Fig and Pumpkin Slice

MAKES 2 LB

1 lb or 450 g pumpkin flesh,
  chopped
4 oz or 100 g chopped figs
4 oz or 100 g chopped dates
4 oz or 100 g gluten-free flour
  mix

4 oz or 100 g caster sugar
1 oz or 25 g melted butter
1 tablespoon honey
1 beaten egg
salt to taste

- Line a shallow 11 × 8 inch/28 × 20 cm tin with foil.
- Mix all the ingredients together and spread over the foil in the tin.
- Bake in a preheated oven, gas mark 4, 350°F, 180°C, for 20–30 minutes until the top is golden brown.
- When cold, cut into fingers and turn out of the tin.

Coconut and Cherry Slices

MAKES 1½ LB

8 oz or 225 g chocolate bar
  (not cooking chocolate)
3 oz or 75 g soft margarine
3 oz or 75 g caster sugar

6 oz or 175 g desiccated coconut
4 oz or 100 g chopped cherries
1 egg

- Line a swiss roll tin with foil or non-stick baking parchment.
- Melt the chocolate by heating very gently in a bowl over a pan of boiling water.
- Pour the chocolate into the lined tin and then cool in the fridge until set.
- Cream the margarine and sugar together, then beat in the egg, desiccated coconut and chopped cherries.
- Spread the mixture to form a layer over the set chocolate.
- Bake at gas mark 4, 350°F, 180°C, for 25–30 minutes or until golden.
- Cool in the tin until cold and then cut into fingers.
- Store in an airtight container.

Mum's Flapjack

MAKES 1½ LB

4 oz or 100 g caster sugar
3 oz or 75 g butter or hard
  margarine
1 tablespoon golden syrup or
  treacle

2 oz or 50 g cornflakes
4 oz or 100 g flaked millet
  (purchased as precooked)
4 oz or 100 g flaked rice
  (purchased as precooked)

- Melt the butter, sugar and syrup together over a low heat until the sugar is dissolved.
- Stir in the cornflakes, millet flake and rice flake.
- Grease a shallow 11 × 8 inch/28 × 20 cm tin.
- Spread the mixture in the tin.
- Bake in a preheated oven, gas mark 2, 300°F, 150°C, for 30–45 minutes until the top is golden brown.
- Cut into fingers when hot and turn out of the tin when cold.

Variations
- Add 2 oz chopped mixed nuts

Meringues

MAKES 16

2 egg whites   1 oz or 25 g granulated sugar
4 oz or 100 g caster sugar

- Cover a large baking ray with non-stick baking parchment.
- Beat the egg whites until stiff.
- Add half the caster sugar and continue beating until the mixture stands in firm peaks.
- Add the remaining caster sugar and continue to beat until the mixture is very stiff and has a silky texture.
- Fold in the granulated sugar.
- Spoon out to make 16 meringues on the prepared sheet.
- Bake at gas mark ¼, 225°F, 110°C, for 2½ hours or until they are crisp and firm. Take care, some ovens will not stay cool enough to make meringues.
- Cool on a wire tray and store in an airtight container.
- Serve sandwiched together in pairs with whipped cream.

Variations
- Add 2 teaspoons instant coffee powder with the granulated sugar.
- Add 2 oz/50 g chopped nuts with the granulated sugar.

Puddings

Baked Rice Pudding

SERVES 4

3 oz or 75 g pudding rice
2 oz or 50 g sugar
1 pint or 550 ml milk

2 eggs
1 drop vanilla essence

- Wash the rice and then boil in one pint water for 5 minutes. Leave to stand for 10 minutes.
- Beat together the sugar, milk and eggs with one drop vanilla essence.
- Drain the rice and add it to the beaten mixture.
- Place the mixture in an ovenproof bowl and sprinkle nutmeg on top.
- Stand the bowl in a tray of water in the oven. The water should come half way up the bowl.
- Bake in a preheated oven, gas mark 4, 350°F, 180°C, for 1½ hours or until just set.

Variations
- Add 2 oz/50 g chocolate (not cooking chocolate), melted in the microwave on low, and beaten into the mixture before baking.

Sweet Rice Dessert

SERVES 4

4 oz or 100 g pudding rice
2 oz or 50 g sugar
1¼ pint or 700 ml milk
1 oz or 25 g butter
1 drop vanilla essence

salt to taste
3 eggs
9 oz or 250 g cooked cooking
  apple

- Wash the rice and then boil in one pint water for 5 minutes. Leave to stand for 10 minutes.
- Beat together the sugar, milk and butter with one drop vanilla essence.
- Drain the rice and add it to the beaten mixture.
- Place in a flameproof and ovenproof bowl and bring quickly to the boil on a high heat.
- Place the bowl in a preheated oven, gas mark 4, 350°F, 180°C, for 30 minutes.
- Beat the eggs.
- Remove the rice from the oven and mix in the beaten eggs.
- Put layers of cooked rice and cooked apple in an ovenproof dish and return to the oven until the top is brown.

Variations
- Many other fruits can be served with rice in this way.

Ground Rice Pudding

SERVES 4

1 pint or 550 ml milk
3 oz or 75 g ground rice
1 oz or 25 g sugar

1 oz or 25 g butter
2 eggs
1 drop vanilla essence

- Bring the milk to the boil and sprinkle in the ground rice, stirring all the time.
- Simmer gently for 20 minutes.
- Allow to cool.

- Beat the sugar, butter and egg together and then mix in the rice, milk, and the vanilla essence.
- Place in an ovenproof bowl.
- Bake in a preheated oven, gas mark 4, 350°F, 180°C, for 1 hour.

Tapioca or Sago Pudding

SERVES 4

1 pint or 550 ml milk	1 drop vanilla essence
3 oz or 75 g sugar	2 oz or 50 g butter
salt to taste	3 eggs
4 oz or 100 g pearl sago or tapioca	1 oz or 25 g butter

- Bring the milk to the boil and stir in the sugar and sago or tapioca together with the salt, vanilla and 2 oz butter.
- When well mixed cook in a preheated oven, gas mark 2, 300°F, 150°C, for 25 minutes.
- Allow to cool.
- Separate the eggs.
- Beat the egg yolks into the cooked sago or tapioca together with the remaining 1 oz butter.
- Beat the egg whites until stiff and fold these into the mixture.
- Stand the bowl in a tray of water in the oven. The water should come half way up the bowl.
- Bake in a preheated oven, gas mark 4, 350°F, 180°C, for 1½ hours or until just set.

Cheesecake

MAKES AN 8 INCH/20 CM CHEESECAKE

For the base
2 pints or 1100 ml puff rice
  cereal
4 oz or 100 g plain chocolate bar

For the topping
½ oz or 11 g gelatine
1 cup very hot water

1½ lb or 700 g cream cheese
  or fromage frais
3 fl oz or 75 ml jam
  or
orange juice and grated orange
rind.

- Melt the chocolate over a low heat in a large pan and stir in the puff rice until all the rice is well covered in chocolate.
- Line the base of a loose bottom 8 inch/20 cm cake tin with baking parchment. Cut another piece of parchment to line the sides. Place the chocolate and puff rice mixture in the base of the tin and press it down gently with a spatula.
- Place the base in the fridge until set.
- Sprinkle the gelatine over a cup of very hot water, stir gently until dissolved.
- Beat the sugar and jam or orange juice into the cream cheese and then beat in all the gelatine solution until smooth.
- Pour the topping mixture onto the prepared base and chill in the fridge until cold.
- Remove from the tin and peel off the baking parchment at the sides before serving.

Variations
- Use any jam and include fresh fruit pieces in the filling.
- Beat in two egg yolks to the filling (note, these are not cooked).
- Use the shortbread recipe to make a different cheesecake base. See page 145 for the recipe.
- Use white chocolate for the rice base.

Apple Soufflé

SERVES 4

6 medium-sized cooking apples   9 oz or 250 g sugar
4 oz or 100 g butter   2 eggs
½ teaspoon ground cinnamon   6 egg yolks
1 oz or 25 g cornflour

- Peel, core and slice the apples and cook in the butter and cinnamon until soft. Liquidise the cooked apple.
- Make the cornflour into a paste with a drop of cold water.
- Stir the sugar and cornflour paste into the apple and continue to cook until the mixture becomes firm.
- Allow the mixture to cool and then beat in the whole eggs and the egg yolks.
- Stand the bowl in a tray of water in the oven. The water should come half way up the bowl.
- Bake in a preheated oven, gas mark 4, 350°F, 180°C, for 1 hour or until just set.

Danish Apple Pudding

SERVES 4

1 lb or 450 g cooking apples   2 oz or 50 g ground almonds
2 oz or 50 g sugar   1 egg
2 oz or 50 g butter or margarine

- Peel and core the apples and cook with the minimum of water (or microwave with no added sugar). Add sugar to taste.
- Cream the butter and sugar together and beat in the almonds. Beat the egg on its own and then beat into the almond mixture.
- Spread the cooked apple in a pie dish and then cover with the almond mixture.
- Bake at gas mark 4, 350°F, 180°C, for 25–35 minutes or until lightly set and golden.
- Serve hot or cold with ice-cream, whipped cream or yogurt.

Chocolate Mousse

Do not use cooking chocolate, use pure plain chocolate bar.

SERVES 4

8 oz or 225 g plain chocolate (**not** cooking chocolate)	4 eggs
¼ pint or 150 ml double cream	1 oz or 25 g sugar
	3 tablespoons rum or brandy

- Separate the eggs.
- Melt the chocolate over a pan of hot, not boiling, water and then stir in the double cream and keep hot.
- Beat together the egg yolks and sugar.
- Add the chocolate mixture gradually to the yolks and sugar and then continue to whisk over the hot water for five minutes until thick and creamy.
- Remove from the heat and add the rum or brandy.
- Whisk the egg whites until stiff and then fold into the mixture.
- Chill and decorate with a little grated chocolate before serving.

Pavlova

SERVES 4

4 egg whites	1 teaspoon lemon juice
pinch salt	2 teaspoons cornflour
8 oz or 225 g caster sugar	2 oz or 50 g walnuts

- Whisk the egg whites and the salt together until stiff.
- Gradually whisk in the sugar until the mixture stands in stiff peaks.
- Then sift the cornflour over the mixture and fold in together with the walnuts and lemon juice.
- Line a tray with non-stick baking parchment and spread the mixture into a circle, leaving a slight hollow in the centre.
- Bake in a preheated oven, gas mark 2, 300°F, 150°C, for 45 minutes–1 hour. Ensure that your oven is not hotter than this.
- Fill the pavlova with whipped cream and decorate with more walnuts and a little grated chocolate.

Lemon Cream

SERVES 4

½ oz or 12 g powdered gelatine
4 fl oz or 150 ml hot water
6 oz or 175 g sugar

2 lemons
2 eggs
½ pint or 280 ml full-cream milk

- Dissolve the gelatine in the water by sprinkling it over 4 fl oz/ 150 ml very hot water. Stir until the gelatine has dissolved.
- Then add the sugar, stirring until all is dissolved.
- Allow to cool until only warm
- Add juice from lemons.
- Separate the eggs.
- Beat the egg yolk and then stir into the warm solution of gelatine and sugar.
- Stir the milk into the mixture, keeping it warm over a gentle heat.
- Remove the mixture from the heat.
- Beat the egg whites and fold this into the mixture.
- Pour the mixture into a serving bowl and place in the fridge until set.
- Prepare in the morning for an evening meal.

Sweet Chestnut Vacherin

SERVES 4

For the meringue
4 egg whites
pinch salt
8 oz or 225 g caster sugar
½ teaspoon vanilla essence
4 oz or 100 g finely ground
  hazelnuts

For the sweet chestnut filling
8 oz or 225 g unsweetened
  tinned chestnut purée
2 oz or 25 g sugar
dark rum to taste (1 measure)
¼ pint or 150 ml double cream
  or fromage frais

- Whisk the egg whites and the salt together until stiff.
- Gradually whisk in the sugar until the mixture stands in stiff peaks.
- Then add the vanilla essence and fold in the finely ground hazelnuts.

157

- Line a tray with non-stick baking parchment and spread the mixture leaving a slight hollow in the centre.
- Bake in a preheated oven, gas mark 2, 300°F, 150°C, for 45 minutes to 1 hour.
- Whisk the sweet chestnut purée with the sugar and rum. Whip the cream separately and then fold the two together.
- Spread the filling on the meringue just before serving.

Chocolate Roll

SERVES 4

8 oz or 225 g plain chocolate
  (not cooking chocolate)
1 tablespoon water

4 eggs, separated
8 oz or 225 g sugar

- Melt the chocolate with the water but do not overheat.
- Whisk the egg yolks with half the sugar until thick and then whisk in the chocolate mixture.
- Whisk the egg whites until stiff and then whisk in the remaining sugar until the mixture stands in peaks.
- Fold the chocolate mixture into the egg whites.
- Grease or line a swiss roll tin and spread the mixture in the tin.
- Bake in a preheated oven, gas mark 4, 350°F, 180°C, for 25–30 minutes or until firm.
- Allow to cool for 5 minutes before covering with a clean damp tea towel and refrigerate overnight.
- Just before serving cover with whipped cream and roll up like a swiss roll.

Sponge Pudding

SERVES 4

2 eggs	6 oz or 175 g gluten-free flour
6 fl oz or 175 ml milk or water	mix
4 oz or 100 g sugar	½ teaspoon cream of tartar
4 oz or 100 g butter	½ teaspoon bicarbonate of soda

- Cream the butter and sugar together until they are light and fluffy.
- In a separate bowl sieve the flours together and mix with the raising agents.
- Beat the eggs and milk gradually into the creamed mixture.
- Fold in the sifted flour.
- Immediately place the mixture in a greased two-pint bowl.
- Cover the bowl with greaseproof paper and aluminium foil and secure with string. Steam for 2 hours.
- **or** cook in a microwave (do not use aluminium foil!) for 4–6 minutes on max (high), turning every 2 minutes. Then stand for 2 minutes before serving.
- **or** preheat oven, gas mark 4, 350°F, 180°C, and bake for 1–1¼ hours.

Variations

SYRUP SPONGE
- Place one large tablespoon syrup in the greased two-pint bowl before adding the mixture.

APRICOT SPONGE
- Place 4 oz/100 g chopped soaked apricots in the greased two-pint bowl before adding the mixture.

MARMALADE SPONGE
- Place one large tablespoon marmalade in the greased two-pint bowl before adding the mixture.

CHOCOLATE SPONGE
- Add 2 teaspoons cocoa powder with the flour.

GINGER SPONGE
- Add 1 teaspoon ginger powder with the flour and 2 oz/50 g chopped preserved ginger.

- You can make a moister sponge pudding by adding 1 large banana or 4 oz/100 g unsweetened, tinned chestnut purée or apple or tofu to the eggs and milk. Beat the banana/sweet chestnut/tofu to a smooth purée with the milk and egg. This is best done in a liquidiser.

Fruit Crumble

SERVES 4

For the topping
6 oz or 175 g gluten-free flour mix
3 oz or 75 g butter or margarine
3 oz or 75 g sugar

For the filling
1½ lb or 700 g peeled and sliced apples, plums, gooseberries or blackcurrants

- Mix all the dry ingredients for the topping together and then rub in the fat until a fine mixture or a soft dough is produced – this will depend on the type of margarine or butter that is used.
- Place the fruit in the bottom of a medium-sized pie dish and sprinkle sugar on the fruit to taste. Most fruit do not need extra water.
- Place the crumble mixture over the fruit in the pie dish.
- Bake in a preheated oven, gas mark 4, 350°F, 180°C, for 30–40 minutes until the top is brown.

Black Forest Trifle

This dish should be prepared on the day it is to be eaten.

SERVES 4–6

8 oz or 225 g gluten-free chocolate cake. See page 120 for the recipe.
6 fl oz or 170 ml kirsch
15 oz or 425 g canned black cherries
5 oz or 150 g black cherry jelly, packet

For the custard
1 oz or 25 g cornflour
1–2 oz or 25–50 g sugar to taste

¾ pint or 425 ml milk
2 tablespoons cocoa powder

For the topping
½ pint or 280 ml whipping cream
1 oz or 25 g plain chocolate, grated (not cooking chocolate)

- Cut the chocolate sponge cake into 1 inch/2.5 cm cubes and place in a glass bowl.
- Pour the kirsch over the cake.
- Drain the cherry juice and keep separately.
- Keep a few cherries to decorate the top and place the remaining cherries over the cake.
- Make up the jelly using the cherry juice and added water, according to the instructions on the packet.
- Pour the liquid jelly (at the point of setting) over the cake and cherries and leave to set.
- **To make the custard**, mix the cornflour, sugar and cocoa powder with a little cold milk into a smooth paste, then add the remaining milk and mix well.
- Heat the custard, stirring continuously, until it reaches a simmer and the custard thickens. Do not boil the custard.
- Pour the custard over the set base and leave to cool.
- When cool cover with whipped cream and grated chocolate and place the remaining cherries on top.
- Keep refrigerated until it is served.

Sticky Chocolate Trifle

This dish should be prepared on the day it is to be eaten.

SERVES 4–6

8 oz or 225 g gluten-free
  chocolate cake. See page 120
  for the recipe.
6 fl oz or 170 ml crème de
  banane or whisky
2 large bananas, sliced

For the custard
4 fl oz or 125 ml can evaporated
  milk
3 oz or 75 g sugar

1 oz or 25 g cornflour
¼ pint or 150 ml milk
3 oz or 75 g plain chocolate
  (not cooking chocolate)

For the topping
½ pint or 280 ml whipping cream
1 oz or 25 g plain chocolate,
  grated

- Cut the chocolate sponge cake into 1 inch/2.5 cm cubes and place in a glass bowl.
- Slice the banana and mix with the cake cubes.
- Pour the *crème de banane* or whisky over the cake and banana.
- **To make the custard**, stir the sugar into the evaporated milk in a pan and stir over a gentle heat until all the sugar as dissolved.
- Bring to a simmer. Simmer gently for 6 minutes.
- Add the 3 oz/75 g plain chocolate broken into small lumps and stir until the chocolate is well mixed in.
- Mix the cornflour with a little cold milk into a smooth paste, then add the remaining milk and mix well.
- Add the cornflour mixture to the chocolate mixture.
- Heat the custard, stirring continuously, until it reaches a simmer and the custard thickens. Do not boil it.
- Pour the custard over the base and leave to cool.
- When cool cover with whipped cream and grated chocolate.
- Keep refrigerated until it is served.

Pear and Ginger Trifle

This dish should be prepared on the day it is to be eaten.

SERVES 4–6

8 oz or 200 g gluten-free
  gingerbread. See page 131 for
  recipe.
6 fl oz or 170 ml ginger wine
15 oz or 425 g canned pears in
  juice.
5 oz or 150 g orange jelly, packet

For the custard
1 oz or 25 g cornflour

1–2 oz or 25–50 g sugar to taste
¾ pint or 425 ml milk
2 teaspoons ground ginger

For the topping
½ pint or 280 ml whipping cream
1 oz or 25 g chopped, crystallised
  stem ginger

- Cut the ginger cake into 1 inch/2.5 cm cubes and place in a glass bowl.
- Pour the wine over the cake.
- Drain the pear juice and keep separately.
- Place the sliced pears over the cake.
- Make up the jelly using the pear juice instead of water, according to the instructions on the packet.
- Pour the liquid jelly (at the point of setting) over the cake and pears and leave to set.
- **To make the custard**, mix the cornflour, sugar and ground ginger with a little cold milk into a smooth paste, then add the remaining milk and mix well.
- Heat the custard, stirring continuously, until it reaches a simmer and the custard thickens. Do not boil it.
- Pour the custard over the set base and leave to cool.
- When cool cover with whipped cream and chopped ginger.
- Keep refrigerated until it is served.

Almond Trifle

This dish should be prepared on the day it is to be eaten.

SERVES 4–6

8 oz or 200 g Bataclan. See
  page 126 for recipe.
6 fl oz or 170 ml peach or
  apricot liqueur.
2 large peaches or apricots, sliced.

For the custard
4 fl oz or 115 ml can evaporated
  milk
3 oz or 75 g sugar
1 oz or 25 g cornflour
¼ pint or 150 ml milk

For the topping
½ pint or 280 ml fresh whipping
  cream
1 oz or 25 g flaked almonds

- Cut the Bataclan sponge cake into 1 inch/2 cm cubes and place in a glass bowl.
- Slice the fruit and mix with the cake cubes.
- Pour the liqueur over the cake and fruit.
- **To make the custard**, stir the sugar into the evaporated milk in a pan and stir over a gentle heat until all the sugar has dissolved.
- Bring to a simmer. Simmer gently for 6 minutes.
- Mix the cornflour with a little cold milk into a smooth paste, then add the remaining milk and mix well.
- Add the cornflour mixture to the evaporated milk mixture.
- Heat the custard, stirring continuously, until it reaches a simmer and the custard thickens. Do not boil the custard.
- Pour the custard over the base and leave to cool.
- When cool cover with whipped cream and almond chips.
- Keep refrigerated until it is served.

Pastry

Shortcrust Potato Pastry

MAKES ½ LB PASTRY

5 oz or 150 g gluten-free flour
  mix
½ teaspoon salt
6 oz or 175 g cooked mashed
  potato

4 oz or 100 g butter or
  margarine
Do not add extra water

- Beat the flour and salt into the potato. A food processor gives the best results. Add the fat, cutting into small pieces with a knife before beating into the flour.
- Work the dough lightly and briefly into a ball, wrap in cling film and refrigerate for 30 minutes.
- Knead the dough on a cold, floured surface (use cornflour) with the heel of the hand for 1–2 minutes when it should be smooth and putty-like.
- Refrigerate for another 30 minutes before rolling out on a cold, floured board to the required shape. Keep moving it round on the board so that it does not stick. I find it easier to roll it out between two sheets of silicone-coated paper.
- Bake empty pastry shells in a preheated oven, gas mark 7, 425°F, 220°C, for 15–20 minutes or until golden brown.

Shortcrust pastry

MAKES ½ LB PASTRY

1 small banana
4 oz or 100 g apple
1 egg yolk
6 oz or 175 g gluten-free flour
  mix

2 tablespoons water
2½ oz or 60 g butter
2½ oz or 60 g lard
½ teaspoon salt

- Beat the banana and apple to a smooth purée with the egg yolk and water. This is best done in a liquidiser.
- Sift the flour and salt into a bowl. Add the fat, cutting into small pieces with a knife before rubbing into the flour to form fine crumbs.
- Mix in the purée using a knife.
- Work the dough lightly and briefly into a ball, wrap in cling film and refrigerate for 30 minutes.
- Flour a cold surface with cornflour. Knead the dough on the cold, floured surface with the heel of the hand for 1–2 minutes when it should be smooth and putty-like.
- Refrigerate for another 30 minutes before rolling out on the cold, floured board to the required shape. Keep moving it round on the board so that it does not stick.
- Bake empty pastry shells in a preheated oven, gas mark 7, 425°F, 220°C, for 15–20 minutes or until brown.

Apple Pie

SERVES 4

8 oz or 225 g shortcrust pastry
dough. See page 167 for
ingredients.

2 lb or 900 g apples
3 oz or 75 g sugar
cloves to taste

- Peel, core and slice 2 lb/900 g apples and place in a 1½ pint pie dish, sprinkling each layer of apples with sugar.
- Make sure that the apples in the centre of the dish are higher than the rim.
- Add one or two cloves if these are liked.
- Roll out the pastry to cover the dish with a slight overlap.
- Brush the edge of the dish with water and place the pastry over the dish and press down to seal the edges.
- Bake in a preheated oven, gas mark 6, 400°F, 200°C, for 40 minutes.

Variations
- Use ¾ lb/325 g ripe brambles (blackberries) to 1¼ lb 550 g apples. Add 2 tablespoons water.
- **Other fruit to use as a filling**: plums, rhubarb, gooseberries. Do not add extra water. Blackcurrants – add 2 tablespoons water.

Pumpkin Pie

SERVES 4

8 oz or 225 g shortcrust potato
pastry
3 eggs
4 oz or 100 g sugar
½ teaspoon ground allspice
½ teaspoon ground cinnamon

¼ teaspoon ground nutmeg
salt to taste
1 lb or 450 g pumpkin purée
½ pint or 280 ml milk
¼ pint or 150 ml whipping cream

- Line the bottom and sides of a shallow 10 inch/25 cm pie dish with the pastry.
- Beat the eggs together with the sugar and spices.
- Beat in the pumpkin purée and then the milk until well mixed.

- Place the mixture in the pie dish.
- Bake in a preheated oven, gas mark 6, 400°F, 200°C, for 40 minutes or until the mixture is set and the top brown.
- Serve hot. Fill the top with whipped cream immediately before serving.

Sunflower Pastry Jam Roll

SERVES 4

2 oz or 50 g ground sunflower
 seeds
1 egg
4 oz or 100 g grated carrot
3 fl oz or 90 ml milk
4 oz or 100 g gluten-free flour
 mix

1 teaspoon bicarbonate of soda
½ teaspoon cream of tartar
1 oz or 25 g sugar
1 oz or 25 g lard or butter

- Grind the sunflower seeds in a liquidiser.
- Blend the carrot to a smooth purée with the milk and egg. This is best done in a liquidiser.
- In a separate bowl sieve together the flour and bicarbonate of soda, cream of tartar and mix with the sugar.
- Then rub in the lard or butter.
- Fold the ground sunflower seeds into the purée.
- Fold the flour mix into the liquid mix.
- Use rice flour when rolling out the pastry.
- Spread the pastry with jam and roll up, sealing the ends with a little pressure.
- Place the pastry roll on non-stick baking parchment on a baking tray.
- Bake in a preheated oven, gas mark 7, 425°F, 220°C, for 15–20 minutes or until golden brown.

Variations
- Spread the pastry with chopped dates before rolling up.
- This pastry can also be used as an excellent pizza base.

Salads

Coleslaw

---

2 apples	1 oz or 25 g parsley
8 oz or 225 g hard white cabbage	1 teaspoon caraway seed
6 oz or 150 g carrot	1 tablespoon olive oil
2 oz or 50 g celery	1 tablespoon vinegar
2 oz or 50 g onion	salt to taste

- Core and dice the apples, slice the cabbage as thinly as possible, slice the celery and onion and grate the carrot.
- Mix all the ingredients together and mix again before serving.
- Vary the proportion of ingredients as you require.

Greek Salad

SERVES 4

4 medium tomatoes	8 black olives
½ cucumber	1 tablespoon olive oil
1 medium onion	1 tablespoon wine vinegar
4 oz or 100 g feta cheese	pinch fresh basil

- Thinly slice the tomato, cucumber and onion and mix with the olive oil and wine vinegar.
- Cut the cheese into small cubes and place on top.
- Scatter the olives on top.
- Sprinkle freshly chopped basil over the salad.

169

Vegetables

Baked Potato/Sweet Potato/Yams
- Medium-sized potatoes are easier to cook than the very large ones.
- Scrub the vegetables and dry them.
- Prick in several places with a fork to prevent them bursting in the oven.
- Bake in a preheated oven, gas mark 5, 375°F, 190°C, until soft.
- Baking time depends on the size of the vegetable, from 40–80 minutes.

Serving suggestions
- Split and spread with garlic butter.
- Grilled cheese – split the cooked hot potato in two and cover with grated cheese, then return to the oven until the cheese has melted.
- Fill will salad and gluten-free mayonnaise. See page 186 for recipe.
- Split and serve with pickles and chutneys.

Potato Chips
- It is not essential to peel the potatoes before cutting into chips.
- If you do want chips without potato skins, scrub the skins clean before peeling potatoes. Deep-fry the skins until gold brown to eat as a snack.
- Yams should be boiled before cutting into chips.
- Cook chips in the oven at 200°C in a little oil in a roasting tin.
- Always have a tight-fitting lid to hand in case of fire if you use a pan.
- Do not allow the oil to get so hot that it produces smoke.

Boiled Potato, Sweet Potato
- These are more nutritious if cooked in their skins. Cooking times depend on the age and the size of the potato. Cover with water and boil for 10–20 minutes. Peeled potatoes are much more likely to break up in the pan.

RICE

- Use long grain rice for savoury dishes and short grain rice for sweet dishes.

Boiled White Rice

- Allow 2 oz/50 g dry rice per person.
- Cover with ½ pint/250 ml water for each 2 oz/50 g portion.
- Boil for 20 minutes until soft but not disintegrating and then drain the rice. The water in which the rice has been boiled can be used to make sauces or soups.
- For a fluffy texture rinse the hot cooked rice well with boiling water.

Boiled Brown Rice

- Cover with ½ pint/250 ml water for each 2 oz/50 g portion.
- Boil for 40 minutes until soft and then drain the rice.
- Brown rice keeps a firmer texture than white rice.

Fried Rice

- Heat 1 tablespoon olive oil for each 2 oz/50 g portion of rice in a large deep frying pan. When the oil is smoking, stir in the rice. Keep over a moderate heat until the rice turns white. Then add ⅓ pint/200 ml water or stock for each 2 oz/50 g rice and simmer until tender.

Millet, Boiled

- Allow 2 oz/50 g dry millet per person.
- Cover with ½ pint/280 ml water for each 2 oz/50 g portion.
- Boil for 40 minutes until soft and then drain the millet.
- Millet keeps a firmer texture than rice.

Quinnoa, Boiled

- Allow 2 oz/50 g dry quinnoa per person.
- Put the grain in a fine sieve and pour a kettle of boiling water through the grain to rinse it well.
- Cover with ¼ pint/150 ml water for each 2 oz/50 g portion.
- Boil for 15 minutes until soft and then drain the quinnoa.

FRESH VEGETABLES

Artichoke – Globe

- Break the stalk away from the base of the artichoke and then trim the sharp points from the leaves.
- Cover the whole vegetable with water in a large pan, putting a plate on top of them to hold them down in the water. Simmer for 45 minutes.
- Stand the cooked artichokes upside-down to drain before serving.
- Each leaf is pulled off by hand so that the fleshy base of the leaf can be eaten. The central choke – the flower bud – is discarded but the fleshy base below that is also eaten.

Artichoke – Jerusalem

- These knobbly root vegetables should be scrubbed clean and then boiled or roasted in the same way as potatoes.

Asparagus

- This should be simply cooked in boiling, salted water for 18 minutes.

Aubergine

- Slice the aubergine thinly and then sprinkle with salt. Leave this to stand for 30 minutes and then rinse off the salt and blot the slices dry with a clean cloth.
- These prepared slices can be fried, stewed or baked.
- They can also be dipped in pea flour and then deep-fried in very hot oil.

Runner Bean, Fresh

- Fresh pods should snap and have a fine texture with the seeds only partly formed. Over-mature pods can be very stringy and fibrous. Slice the pods before boiling for 10–15 minutes.

French Bean, Fresh

- Use pods that are firm but thin, before the seeds have fully formed. Although they can be sliced, they are best cooked whole. Simmer in boiling water for 10–15 minutes.

Broad Bean, Fresh

- These beans are best when the size of a thumb nail.
- Boil for 10 minutes and drain before serving. Mature but fresh broad beans take up to 20 minutes to cook and have a much coarser texture. They are best used in soups or stews.

Beetroot

- Beetroot should not be peeled or have the leaves cut off before cooking. Remove the leaf stalks by twisting and cover the roots with water.
- Bring to the boil and simmer for 30–40 minutes depending on the size of the roots.
- Allow to cool and the skins can then be removed by rubbing.
- Slice the cooked roots and sprinkle with vinegar or serve hot with white sauce.

Brassicas, Cabbage

- All the brassicas can be eaten raw.
- Cut the leaves into narrow shreds. Use the minimum quantity of water needed to cover the vegetables and bring to the boil. Always aim to cook for the minimum time and serve as soon as the desired texture is reached. 10 15 minutes is often sufficient. Drain well before serving.

Brussels Sprouts

- Trim the base of the stem and remove any damaged outer leaves. Boil for 7–8 minutes before draining and serving. They are easily over cooked.

Cauliflower and Broccoli

- Remove any old and damaged leaves, but any young leaves should be kept.
- Turn the cauliflower upside-down and split the stem from the base to separate the head into portions.
- Place in a pan with the head upwards and cover with water.
- Boil for 15–20 minutes until the stem is tender.

Carrots

- Carrots should be scraped clean. They can be eaten raw, grated in salad or with a dip.

- Carrots can be cooked whole but should not be cut too small unless for soups and stews. Cooking time depends on the age of the carrot. Young carrots take 10–15 minutes in boiling water. Mature carrots take 20 minutes in boiling water.

Jellied Carrots

- Grated raw carrot can be stirred into a jelly made with gelatine and orange juice. This is refrigerated until set and then served cold with cold meat and salad.

Celery

- Eat raw with salad or cut the stem into short lengths and boil for 10–15 minutes until tender. Serve with a white sauce.

Celeriac

- Peel and then dice the root. Boil for 10–15 minutes until tender, then drain and toss in a lump of butter.

Courgettes

- Small courgettes should be cooked whole. Larger should be sliced.
- Boil vigorously for 2 minutes before draining.
- Add one pinch mixed herbs and 1 oz/25 g butter or olive oil to the pan and simmer gently for 15–20 minutes.

Cucumber

- Serve raw in salads.
- Peel and cut into chunks. Boil vigorously for 2 minutes before draining. Add 1 oz/25 g butter to the pan and simmer gently for 5 minutes until tender.

Leeks

- Leeks often contain earth between the leaves. Cut away and discard any dark green part of the leaves.
- Cut away all roots without removing the base of the stem. Now cut from just behind the base of the leek up through the ends of the leaves. Repeat this so that the leek is quartered but still held at the base. The leek can now be well washed in cold water.

- Place in a pan with the minimum of cold water needed to cover and bring to the boil. Simmer for 15 minutes. Leeks can also be cooked by simmering in wine or stock and served in the liquid.

Marrows, Squashes, Pumpkins

- As a simple vegetable, cut in half and remove the seeds. Peel and cut into chunks.
- Boil vigorously for 2 minutes before draining. Add 1 oz/25 g butter to the pan and simmer gently until tender. The time needed depends on the variety and the maturity of the squash.

Onions

- Make sure that any brown skin is removed from the onion. Sliced onion can be fried or boiled for 10 minutes. Whole onions can be boiled for 20 minutes or baked for 30 minutes.

Parsnip

- Peel and cut into large chunks. Place around a joint to be roasted in the oven and turn a couple of times while cooking. Parsnips can also be boiled until tender, for 15–20 minutes.

Peas, Fresh

- Small young peas should be boiled for 10 minutes. Older peas may need from 15–20 minutes boiling until they are tender.

Sweet Corn

- Cut away any extra stalk and remove all the leaves that cover the corn. Cover with water and boil. Young corn may be ready in 5 minutes. More mature corn may take 20 minutes. Drain well and serve with melted butter.

Sweet Potato

- Cook and serve in a similar way to ordinary potato.

Turnip and Swede

- The root should be peeled. Mature roots have a thick skin that should be removed. Mature roots may be very hard when raw

175

and care should be taken when cutting them. Cut into chunks or slices and cover with water. Boil for 20 minutes until soft.

DRIED PEAS AND BEANS

Large quantities of food prepared from dried peas and beans can be indigestible. Limit your intake to 1–2 oz/25 g–50 g dry measure per person per day.

Lentils

- Lentils do not need to be soaked before cooking. They become soft and break up when cooked, so they are best used in soups and stews.

Black-eye Beans

- Soak overnight in twice their own volume of water.
- Drain and cover with fresh water. Bring slowly to the boil and boil rapidly for 10 minutes. Then simmer for 1 hour.

Chick Peas

- Soak overnight in twice their own volume of water.
- Drain and cover with fresh water. Bring slowly to the boil and boil rapidly for 10 minutes. Then simmer for 2 hours.

Mung Beans

- Soak overnight in twice their own volume of water.
- Drain and cover with fresh water. Bring slowly to the boil and simmer for 1 hour. Split mung beans do not need soaking before use.

Haricot beans

- Soak overnight in twice their own volume of water.
- Drain and cover with fresh water. Bring slowly to the boil and boil rapidly for 10 minutes. Then simmer for 1½ hours.

Red Kidney Beans

- Soak overnight in twice their own volume of water.
- Drain and cover with fresh water. Bring slowly to the boil and

boil rapidly for 30 minutes. Discard the water and cover with fresh water, then simmer for 4 hours.

Pigeon Peas

- Soak overnight in twice their own volume of water.
- Drain and cover with fresh water. Bring slowly to the boil and simmer for 1 hour.

Vegetarian dishes

Vegetarian Moussaka

SERVES 4

4 oz or 100 g red lentils
¼ pint or 150 ml water
8 oz or 200 g tomatoes
8 oz or 200 g aubergine
1 clove garlic
1 onion

2 tablespoons olive oil
½ teaspoon mixed herbs
1 egg
6 oz or 150 g soft cheese or
   fromage frais

- Slice the aubergine thinly and then sprinkle with salt. Leave this to stand for 30 minutes and then rinse off the salt and blot the slices dry with a clean cloth.
- Cook the lentils and herbs in ¼ pint/150 ml water for 30 minutes.
- Fry the aubergines, tomatoes, onion and garlic in the oil until soft.
- Mix the cooked lentils with the rest of the vegetables and place in an ovenproof bowl.
- Beat the egg and cheese together and pour over the top.
- Bake in a preheated oven, gas mark 6, 400°F, 200°C, for 20–25 minutes.

Nut Loaf

SERVES 4

1 oz or 25 g vegetable oil
8 oz or 225 g onion, chopped
2 cloves garlic, crushed
5 oz or 150 g gluten-free
  breadcrumbs

8 oz or 225 g chopped hazelnuts
2 eggs
¼ pint or 150 ml water
herbs to taste; sprig rosemary
salt to taste

- Chop and fry the onion and garlic in the oil briefly until soft.
- Mix the chopped nuts and breadcrumbs in a food processor.
- Mix the breadcrumbs, nuts and onion together.
- Beat the eggs, herbs, seasoning and water into the mixture.
- Place the mixture in a greased and lined 1 lb bread tin.
- Bake in a preheated oven, gas mark 6, 400°F, 200°C, for 45–60 minutes.
- Serve hot or cold with a salad.

Dhal

SERVES 4

8 oz or 225 g lentils
1 pint or 550 ml water
½ teaspoon chilli powder
½ teaspoon ground turmeric
½ teaspoon dried fenugreek leaves
½ teaspoon salt

2 oz or 50 g olive oil or clarified
  butter
1 onion
1 clove garlic
1 teaspoon grated fresh ginger

- Bring the lentils to the boil in the water and then add the chilli, turmeric, fenugreek and salt.
- Simmer until cooked, about 45 minutes.
- Chop and fry the onion, garlic and ginger in the oil briefly until soft and then add to the dhal just before serving.
- Serve as a dip with any gluten-free bread, or serve as a vegetable.

Dolmades

SERVES 4

4 fl oz or 125 ml olive oil
2 medium onions
4 oz or 100 g long grain rice
½ pint or 280 ml water
2 oz or 50 g sultanas or currants

½ oz or 10 g fresh mint
½ oz or 10 g parsley
½ teaspoon mixed spice
vine leaves

- Chop the onions and cook gently in the oil until soft.
- Add the rice and continue cooking and stirring until the rice is translucent.
- Add the water and return to the boil.
- Chop the parsley and mint and then add with the remaining ingredients and simmer until the water is absorbed. Check that the rice is cooked at this stage. If not add a little more water and continue to cook until it is soft.
- Plunge the vine leaves into boiling water for 3 minutes and then drain. Place one small spoonful rice in the middle of each vine leaf and roll up into a loose parcel.
- Oil a saucepan and pack the parcels in tightly together.
- Add just enough water to cover the vine leaf parcels and simmer for 1 hour, adding more water if required.
- Allow to go cold before removing from the pan.
- Serve chilled as a starter or a snack.

Hummus

SERVES 4

8 oz or 225 g chick peas	1 teaspoon salt
1 pint or 550 ml water	6 oz or 150 g sesame seeds
3 lemons	2 tablespoons olive oil
5 cloves garlic	paprika to taste

- Soak the chick peas overnight in 1 pint/550 ml water. Drain and wash the peas.
- Place the chick peas in 1 pint fresh water and boil gently for 2 hours or until tender.
- Drain the peas.
- Place the sesame seeds, garlic, olive oil, and half the lemon juice in a blender and reduce to a smooth purée.
- Add the cooked chick peas a few at a time to the mixture in the blender, together with the remaining lemon juice, and reduce to a smooth purée.
- Add a small amount of paprika to produce a spicy taste if required.
- Serve with thin buckwheat pancakes.

Leek and Orange Loaf

SERVES 4

1½ lb or 700 g prepared leeks.
  See page 174.
4 oranges
4 oz or 100 g softened butter
6 medium eggs

salt to taste
fresh ground black pepper to
  taste
2 tablespoons finely chopped
  parsley

- Slice the oranges and simmer them gently in their own juice (you may need to add a little water).
- Liquidise the cooked oranges.
- Split and chop the leeks.
- Cook the leeks in hot sizzling butter until golden and soft.
- Mix the leeks with the oranges.
- Separate the eggs.
- Beat in the egg yolks one at a time to the leek and orange.
- Add the salt, pepper and parsley.
- Beat the egg whites with a pinch of salt until stiff.
- Fold half the egg white into the mixture and then fold in the other half.
- Gently spread the mixture in a shallow greased tin.
- Bake in a preheated oven, gas mark 4, 350°F, 180°C, for 25 minutes.
- Sprinkled with grated cheese and top with yoghurt.

Sauces

Brown Gravy

Do not use gravy browning or stock cubes unless you are sure they do not contain gluten.

- Save the juice in which meat has been roasted or pot roasted.
- Spoon the fat from the surface of the meat juice. Keep the fat for making crispbread.
- Allow the remaining juices to cool.
- Mix one level tablespoon cornflour into a paste with a little cold water.
- Gradually add the meat juices to the cornflour paste, stirring continuously.
- Add enough vegetable water or stock to make the volume of gravy up to ½ pint/280 ml.
- Bring the gravy back to a simmer and simmer for 5 minutes.
- Season with salt and fresh pepper to taste before serving.

Variations

ONION GRAVY
- Chop a medium-sized onion and fry in a little dripping until golden brown. Add this to the gravy

Simple White Sauce

1 oz or 25 g cornflour　　　　*salt and pepper to taste*
½ pint or 280 ml milk

- Mix the cornflour into a paste with a little *cold* milk.
- Stir in the remaining milk without heating.
- Now slowly heat the sauce to simmer, stirring continuously.
- Simmer very gently for 5 minutes.

Variations

CHEESE SAUCE
- Stir 4 oz/100 g grated cheese into the cooked sauce.

ONION SAUCE
- Peel, chop and fry one onion until tender. Stir the cooked onion into the cooked sauce.

PARSLEY SAUCE
- Add one heaped tablespoon chopped parsley to the cooked sauce.

RICH WHITE SAUCE
- Stir 2 oz/50 g butter into the cooked sauce.

Bechamel Sauce

1 oz or 25 g butter	1 oz or 25 g chopped onion
1 oz or 25 g cornflour	1 bay leaf
½ pint or 280 ml milk	

- Melt the butter in a heavy pan then whisk in the flour and cook for several minutes, stirring continuously.
- Bring the milk to the boil and whisk into the butter and flour, stirring continuously.
- Add the chopped onion and the bay leaf.
- Simmer very gently for up to 1 hour.
- Serve with vegetables, fish or eggs.

Variations

MORNAY SAUCE
- For vegetables, fish, poultry and eggs. To the cooked sauce add ¼ pint/150 ml single cream and 2 oz/50 g grated cheese.

Hollandaise Sauce

A traditional rich sauce.

6 oz or 175 g butter	juice half lemon
1½ fl oz or 45 ml water	salt and pepper to taste
3 egg yolks	

- Melt the butter in a heavy pan and allow to cool until just warm but still liquid.
- Warm the water until tepid and then blend the egg yolks, water, salt and pepper in a blender for about 10 seconds.
- Add the warm butter gradually, blending continuously.
- The sauce should thicken.
- Stir in the lemon juice and serve with vegetables, fish or eggs.

Variations

CAPER SAUCE
• For boiled fish, add 2 teaspoons capers.

MOUSSELINE SAUCE
• For fish or boiled vegetables, add 4 fl oz/100 ml whipped cream before serving.
• These sauces should be freshly made and not be kept.
• Note that the egg yolks are not cooked.

Mayonnaise

Do not use mustard powder. It may contain wheat flour.

2 teaspoons sugar	2 tablespoons vinegar
1 teaspoon fresh ground mustard seed	2 tablespoons water
½ teaspoon salt	1 egg

• Beat the ingredients together and then stir continuously in a double boiler over heat until thickened. Do not overcook.
• Keep refrigerated.
• Use within a couple of days
• Note that the egg is not fully cooked.

Italian Tomato Sauce

⅛ pint or 75 ml olive oil
1 onion
2 cloves garlic
2 lb or 1 kg tomato, or one tin
 chopped tomato
1 carrot

1 celery stick
1 oz or 25 g sugar
fresh ground black pepper to
 taste
salt to taste

- Cook the chopped onion and garlic slowly in the oil until soft.
- Add the other ingredients, finely chopped, and simmer gently for at least 1 hour until the sauce is thickening.
- Liquidise before serving.

Indonesian Barbecue Sauce

4 oz or 100 g coconut, fresh or
 desiccated
1 onion

¼ pint or 150 ml milk
½ teaspoon chilli powder to taste
juice one lemon

- Finely chop the coconut and onion.
- Mix all the ingredients together and cook very gently until the onion is soft. This sauce can also be served without cooking.

Mint Sauce

½ oz or 12 g fresh mint leaves
2 tablespoons vinegar

½ oz or 12 g sugar

- Chop the fresh young spearmint or applemint leaves finely. Add the vinegar and sugar and leave to stand for 30 minutes. Stir occasionally.
- Serve with roast lamb.

Garlic Butter

4 oz or 100 g butter
2 cloves garlic

salt to taste
½ oz or 10 g chives

- Warm the butter slightly and then beat into a cream.
- Use a pestle and mortar to grind the garlic with the salt into a paste, and then beat into the creamed butter.
- Gently mix in the chives.
- Refrigerate until ready to serve.

Black Butter

4 oz or 100 g butter
1 tablespoon chopped parsley

1 teaspoon capers
1 tablespoon vinegar

- Heat the butter until it becomes brown (not black).
- Add the chopped parsley and capers to the hot butter.
- Immediately before serving stir the vinegar into the hot butter.
- Serve hot.

Horseradish Sauce

1 oz or 25 g fresh horseradish
2 tablespoons vinegar

¼ pint or 125 ml double cream
salt to taste

- Grate the fresh horseradish and mix with the vinegar and salt.
- Whip the cream and then fold into the mixture.
- Refrigerate until ready to serve.
- Serve with roast beef, beef stews, smoked fish.

Sweet White Sauce

1 oz or 25 g cornflour   1 oz or 25 g sugar
½ pint or 280 ml milk

- Mix the cornflour and sugar into a paste with a little *cold* milk.
- Stir in the remaining milk without heating.
- Now slowly heat the sauce to simmer, stirring continuously.
- Simmer very gently for 5 minutes.

Variations

RICH WHITE SAUCE
- Stir 2 oz/50 g butter into the cooked sauce.

BRANDY SAUCE
- Stir 1–2 tablespoons brandy into the cooked sauce.

CHOCOLATE SAUCE
- Mix 1–2 teaspoons cocoa powder or gluten-free drinking chocolate with the cornflour before adding the cold milk. Add an extra ounce sugar.
- A thick chocolate sauce can be served hot or cold on its own or with bananas as a pudding.

EGG CUSTARD
- Beat 2 eggs into the cold mixture before heating. Heat the custard over a very low flame, stirring continuously while it thickens. Do not let it boil but keep it warm for 3 minutes over the heat. It can be easier to place the pan of custard over another pan of boiling water while it is being heated. It must be stirred all the time.
- Note that the eggs are not fully cooked in egg custard.

Clear Jam Sauce

2 oz or 50 g cornflour	1 oz or 25 g sugar
½ pint or 280 ml water	2 oz or 50 g jam

- Mix the cornflour and sugar into a paste with a little *cold* water.
- Stir in the remaining water and the jam without heating.
- Now slowly heat the sauce to simmer, stirring continuously.
- Simmer very gently for 5 minutes.

Variations
- Allow to cool and set and serve as a cold jelly, or pour over fresh fruit and serve cold.

Rich Custard

This dish should be prepared on the day it is to be eaten.

SERVES 4

4 fl oz or 115 ml can evaporated milk	1 oz or 25 g cornflour
	¼ pint or 150 ml milk
3 oz or 75 g sugar	

- Stir the sugar into the evaporated milk in a pan and stir over a gentle heat until all the sugar has dissolved.
- Bring to a simmer. Simmer gently for 6 minutes.
- Mix the cornflour with a little cold milk into a smooth paste, then add the remaining milk and mix well.
- Add the cornflour mixture to the evaporated milk mixture.
- Heat the custard, stirring continuously, until it reaches a simmer and the custard thickens. Do not boil the custard.

Jelly and jam

Gooseberry and Strawberry Jam

MAKES 8 LB JAM

2 lb or 1 kg gooseberries
2 lb or 1 kg strawberries

4 lb or 2 kg sugar
¼ pint or 150 ml water

- Reduce the quantities in proportion if you do not have a large jam pan.
- Top and tail the gooseberries and remove any stems from the strawberries.
- Put the fruit and water in a large jam pan and simmer until tender.
- Add the sugar and continue to simmer, stirring slowly until all the sugar is dissolved.
- Place eight jam jars in a slow oven (gas mark ½ 250°F/120°C) to heat up.
- Boil rapidly until setting point is reached. (This is 220°F/105°C measured with a sugar thermometer.)
- Test for setting point by removing a few drops of jam and letting cool. Push the cooled jam with a finger. If a skin crinkles on top of the cooled jam then setting point is reached.
- Ladle the jam into the hot jars. A small jug makes this job easier.
- Fill the jars right to the top and cover straight away with plastic covers. These can be cut from thin high density polythene freezer bags.
- Secure the covers with rubber bands and store in a cool cupboard.

Plum Jam

MAKES 8 LB JAM

4 lb or 2 kg plums   ¼ pint or 150 ml water
4 lb or 2 kg sugar

- Reduce the quantities in proportion if you do not have a large jam pan.
- Put the fruit and water in a large jam pan and simmer until tender. Then allow to cool.
- Squeeze the plums through your fingers into a bowl, retaining the stones with the fingers. Discard the stones.
- Add the sugar to the plums and bring back to simmer, stirring slowly until all the sugar is dissolved.
- Place eight jam jars in a slow oven (gas mark ½ 250°F/120°C) to heat up.
- Boil rapidly until setting point is reached. (This is 220°F/105°C measured with a sugar thermometer.)
- Test for setting point by removing a few drops of jam and letting cool. Push the cooled jam with a finger. If a skin crinkles on top of the cooled jam then setting point is reached.
- Ladle the jam into the hot jars. A small jug makes this job easier.
- Fill the jars right to the top and cover straight away with plastic covers. These can be cut from thin high density polythene freezer bags.
- Secure the covers with rubber bands and store in a cool cupboard.

Pickles

Green Tomato Chutney

MAKES **10** LB CHUTNEY

2 lb or 1 kg green tomatoes	1 lb 6 oz or 1.5 kg sugar
3 pints or 2 litres distilled	1 oz or 25 g salt
vinegar (extra strength)	2 oz or 50 g ground ginger
2 lb or 1 kg large cooking apples	2 oz or 50 g fresh ground
2 lb or 1 kg onions	mustard seed
3 cloves garlic	1 teaspoon allspice
2 lb or 1 kg sultanas	1 teaspoon ground cinnamon

- Core the apples and remove any brown skin from the onions.
- Chop the apples, onions, tomatoes, sultanas and garlic. Add all the remaining ingredients and simmer for 1–2 hours.
- Heat the jars in a slow oven.
- Ladle the chutney into the jars and fill to the top and cover straight away with plastic covers. These can be cut from thin high density polythene freezer bags. Secure the covers with rubber bands and make second covers over the top with aluminium foil.
- Store in a cool cupboard.
- Keep for at least 1 month before using.

Home-made sweets

Almond Brittle

This is a traditional recipe.

MAKES 2 LB BRITTLE

1 lb or 450 g blanched, chopped
  almonds
14 oz or 400 g sugar

juice one lemon
1¼ pints or 750 ml water

- To blanch almonds: Pour boiling water over the almonds and leave them to stand in the water for 2 minutes. The brown skins are then easily rubbed off.
- Use a heavy pan and a long wooden spoon.
- Dissolve the sugar in the water. Do not let it boil until all the sugar has dissolved, then boil vigorously, stirring with a wooden spoon, until the sugar thermometer shows the temperature to be 290°F/145°C.
- Take off the heat.
- Take care not to splash the mixture which is very hot.
- Stir in the almonds and the juice from the lemon.
- The texture changes rapidly at this point. Continue to stir until well mixed.
- Then pour the mixture onto a greased tray to cool.
- Cut into small squares when cold and store in an airtight container.

Variations

SESAME BRITTLE
- Use 1 lb hulled sesame seed in place of almonds.

Coffee Caramel

MAKES 1½ LB RICH, CREAMY CARAMEL

13 oz or 350 g sugar
1 pint or 550 ml double cream
4 oz or 100 g corn syrup

4 oz or 100 g butter
½ oz or 12 g instant coffee powder

- Stir all the time that the mixture is being heated.
- Use a large, heavy pan.
- Dissolve the sugar and syrup in the cream and boil vigorously, stirring with a wooden spoon, until the sugar thermometer shows the temperature to be 265°F/130°C.
- Take off the heat.
- Take care not to splash the mixture which is very hot.
- Stir in the coffee powder and then stir in the butter a little at a time.
- Then pour the mixture onto a greased tray to cool.
- Cut in small squares when cold and store in an airtight container.

Variations
- Add 2 oz/50 g chopped nuts to the cooked hot mixture before pouring onto the greased tray.

Treacle Toffee

MAKES 1 LB OF TOFFEE

8 oz or 225 g brown sugar
8 oz or 225 g treacle

2 oz or 50 g butter
1 fl oz or 30 ml vinegar

- Stir all the time that the mixture is being heated.
- Use a large, heavy pan.
- Dissolve the sugar and treacle in the vinegar and boil vigorously, stirring with a wooden spoon, until the sugar thermometer shows the temperature to be 284°F/142°C. Take care not to splash the mixture which is very hot.
- Take off the heat.
- Stir in the butter a little at a time.
- Then pour the mixture onto a greased tray to cool.

- Break into small squares when cold and store in an airtight container.

Variations
- More butter can be added to make a richer toffee.

Treacle Fudge

MAKES 1½ LB FUDGE

1 lb or 450 g brown sugar	2 oz or 50 g butter
4 oz or 100 g treacle	½ pint or 280 ml milk

- Stir all the time that the mixture is being heated.
- Use a large heavy pan.
- Dissolve the sugar and treacle in the milk and boil vigorously, stirring with a wooden spoon, until the sugar thermometer shows the temperature to be 240°F/115°C. Take care not to splash the mixture which is very hot.
- Take off the heat.
- Stir in the butter a little at a time.
- Turn out as soon as a fudge consistency is reached.
- Then pour the mixture into a greased 8 inch/20 cm square tin to cool.
- Cut into small squares when cold and store in an airtight container.

Variations
- Add 2 oz/50 g nuts after adding the butter.
       Or
- Add 2 oz/50 g honey to the sugar.
       Or
- Add 2 oz/50 g chocolate bar to the sugar.
  Problems: Most problems result from inaccurate temperatures.
- If the fudge consistency does not develop on cooling, try keeping for a week.
- If fudge has not developed by then, reheat the mixtures and allow to cool again.

Carrot Fudge

MAKES 1 LB FUDGE

¼ pint or 150 ml condensed milk
4 oz or 100 g sugar
1 oz or 25 g golden syrup
3 oz or 75 g butter

2 oz or 50 g sultanas
8 oz or 225 g grated carrot
(flavouring if liked)

- Stir all the time that the mixture is being heated.
- Use a large, heavy pan.
- Dissolve the sugar and syrup in the milk and add the grated carrot and any flavouring. Boil vigorously, stirring with a wooden spoon, until the sugar thermometer shows the temperature to be 240°F/115°C. Take care not to splash the mixture which is very hot.
- Take off the heat.
- Stir in the butter a little at a time.
- Stir in the sultanas.
- Then pour the mixture into a greased 8 inch/20 cm square tin to cool.
- Cut into small squares when cold and store in an airtight container.

Flavourings
- 2 oz or 50 g melted plain chocolate
  - or
- 1 teaspoon cocoa powder
  - or
- 1 teaspoon instant coffee powder
  - or
- I tablespoon orange juice
  - or
- 2 drops vanilla essence

Halva

---

1 lb or 450 g flesh of summer squash, young pumpkin or courgette, peeled with seeds removed	3 cardamom pods
	1 tablespoon crushed sesame seed
	1 tablespoon chopped pistachios
	5 tablespoons sugar
¾ pint or 425 ml whole milk	2 tablespoons olive oil

- Purée the squash flesh and then mix with the milk and cardamom pods in a pan.
- Add the crushed sesame seed and chopped pistachios.
- Now slowly heat the sauce to simmer and then turn the heat down.
- Simmer very gently.
- Stir at intervals until all the liquid has evaporated.
- Add the oil and sugar and continue stirring over the heat for 10 minutes.
- Spread the mixture on non-stick baking parchment on a shallow baking tray.
- Allow to cool before cutting into small cubes and serving.

Marsh Mallow

MAKES 1 LB

8 oz or 225 g sugar	½ oz or 15 g gelatine
2 teaspoons liquid glucose	1 egg white
8 fl oz or 230 ml water	

- Dissolve the gelatine in a further 2 fl oz/75 ml water by sprinkling the powdered gelatine over the very hot water and then stirring until the gelatine has dissolved.
- Whisk the egg white separately until stiff.
- Dissolve the sugar and liquid glucose slowly in the water in a large pan.
- After the sugar is dissolved heat more strongly and boil until a sugar thermometer shows 121°C/250°F.
- Remove the syrup from the heat and with great care gradually add the dissolved gelatine to the syrup. The syrup will bubble up.

- Pour the syrup and gelatine mixture onto the beaten egg white and continue to beat until the mixtures is thick and stiff. This may take several minutes of beating. An electric whisk is very useful for this.
- Pour this stiff mixture into a greased baking tin and allow to cool and set.
- Cut the marsh mallow into squares and dust tops with icing sugar. Use a spatula to lift each square from the tray and dust all other surfaces with icing sugar.

Drinks

Do not drink beer, ale, lager, barley drinks. Check all manufactured drinks.

Fruit Wine

MAKES **1** GALLON WINE

4 lb or 1.8 kg plums
  or elderberries
  or blackcurrants
  or blackberries or rowan

1 oz or 25 g citric acid
3 lb or 1.3 kg sugar
general purpose wine yeast and
  nutrient

- Simmer the fruit very gently in one gallon water for 2 hours. The fruit should not break but their colour should be extracted by the water.
- Strain the liquid into a clean, wide-mouthed container, preferably of glass or food grade plastic, to use as a fermenting jar. The fruit pulp can be eaten.
- Transfer the liquid back into the pan and bring back to simmer.
- Stir in 2 lb/1 kg sugar, continuing to stir until it has all dissolved.
- Stir in the citric acid.
- Return the liquid to the fermenting jar and when it has cooled to 92°F/37°C stir in the yeast and nutrient.
- Cover the fermenting jar with a sheet of clean polythene (from an unused white carried bag) and secure with an elastic band.
- Leave the jar close to a radiator or in a warm cupboard for the contents to ferment for a fortnight. If the contents are fermenting the polythene will be pushed up in a dome by the gas escaping round the edges.
- After a fortnight's fermentation **gradually** stir in 8 oz/225 g sugar. Replace the polythene cover and leave in a warm place to continue fermenting for another fortnight.
- After the second fortnight's fermentation **gradually** stir in 8 oz/225 g sugar. Replace the polythene cover and leave in a

warm place to continue fermenting. It can be left in this jar for up to one year before bottling the wine.

- Decant the wine into clean wine bottles. I wash them in boiling water and then place them in a low oven to sterilise them rather than using chemicals. Let them cool slowly before filling with wine.
- Corks are not needed on wine bottles. Cover the top of each bottle with a square of high density polythene (unused food carrier bags) and secure with an elastic band. The wine will keep well for many years and there is no risk of pressure building up from secondary fermentation.
- Store the bottle upright.
- Decant each bottle slowly before serving to ensure that the dregs to not mix with the wine. Always aim to produce a dry wine – all the sugar used in the fermentation.
- If you require a sweet wine to drink add a little sugar to the decanted wine before serving.

Elderflower Wine

MAKES 1 GALLON WINE.

1 bucket elderflowers (flower stalks do not matter – this is a very approximate quantity)	3 lb or 1.3 kg sugar
	1 pot of tea
	general purpose wine yeast and
1 oz or 25 g citric acid	nutrient

- Simmer the flowers very gently in one gallon water for 2 hours.
- Strain the liquid into a clean, wide-mouthed container, preferably of glass or food grade plastic to use as a fermenting jar.
- Transfer the liquid back into the pan and bring back to simmer.
- Stir in 2 lb/1 kg sugar, continuing to stir until it has all dissolved.
- Stir in the citric acid and pour in the liquid from the pot of tea.
- Return the liquid to the fermenting jar and when it has cooled to 92°F/37°C stir in the yeast and nutrient.
- Cover the fermenting jar with a sheet of clean polythene (from an unused white carried bag) and secure with an elastic band.
- Leave the jar close to a radiator or in a warm cupboard for the contents to ferment for a fortnight. If the contents are fermenting the polythene will be pushed up in a dome by the gas escaping round the edges.

- After a fortnight's fermentation **gradually** stir in 8 oz/225 g sugar. Replace the polythene cover and leave in a warm place to continue fermenting for another fortnight.
- After the second fortnight's fermentation **gradually** stir in 8 oz/225 g sugar. Replace the polythene cover and leave in a warm place to continue fermenting. It can be left in this jar for up to one year before bottling the wine.
- Decant the wine into clean wine bottles following the same instruction as for Fruit Wine.

Mulled Wine

SERVES 20 GLASSES

To 1 litre carton orange juice add:
3 lemons, remove the pips and slice thinly
1 cinnamon stick
10 cloves

½ teaspoon nutmeg
½ teaspoon mixed spices
½ teaspoon allspice
sugar to taste

- Simmer gently for 20 minutes.
- Add 1 litre red wine, elderberry or bramble or a fruity grape wine. Do not boil.
- Serve hot.
- For a non-alcoholic mulled drink add 1 litre apple juice instead of the wine. Do not add sugar until you have tasted the mixture as this is quite sweet.

Freezing

A large deep freeze greatly simplifies catering for a gluten-free household.

Make sure that everything is well labelled. This particularly applies to anything that may not be gluten-free.

If you have to buy grain and flour in bulk, keep all but your immediate needs in the deep-freeze. Place the bags or boxes in which they are supplied within stronger polythene bags and keep them sealed. They will remain pest-free and keep for over a year in this way.

All the bread, rolls, scones, pancakes and cakes in the recipe book freeze well.

We devote a morning at a time to baking and always make quantities that will fill the oven. Anything that we do not want to eat that day is frozen as soon as it is cool.

Only rich fruit cakes and Christmas puddings are kept in a cool larder to mature. This means that we always have a selection of baking available for our meals.

Stocks for soups and stews also freeze well, but it may help to boil them down to reduce the volume. We make use of large yogurt containers for holding these.

We grow many of our own vegetables and soft fruit. Much of the surplus is frozen until it is required. Plain stewed fruit from the freezer has become a staple diet for breakfast or pudding in this household.

The coeliac condition

The human body's immune system is designed to recognise any foreign material in the body and start up a complicated series of events to remove it. Normally this system recognises foreign material like viruses, bacteria or a thorn in the skin. The defence mechanisms then destroy these and protect us from further infection.

This defence mechanism also monitors the uptake of digested food in the small intestine. Starches, sugars and fats are simple molecules and present no problem to this system. The more complex proteins may be recognised as foreign and stimulate the immune system, particularly if the lining of the small intestine has suffered slight damage and the protein is being absorbed in an undigested state.

Gluten is a mixture of complex protein found in the grain of wheat. Similar proteins are found in barley, rye and, to a smaller extent, in oats. It is also found in the wild relatives of these grains, such as spelt.

Gluten is recognised as a foreign substance by the lining of the small intestine in some people. This results in an immune response: inflammation with swelling and soreness. Over a period of time the lining of the small intestine breaks down and loses the tiny villi that absorb the food. This is the coeliac condition.

Once this has happened the only cure is to avoid all food that contains gluten. The immune system remembers all past foreign material and will respond rapidly to a recurrence of the invasion.

Symptoms of the immune response to gluten can range from a feeling of heaviness after a meal to persistent diarrhoea and abdominal swelling and pain. The damage to the small intestine can then result in weight loss and many other symptoms linked to the poor absorption of food, such as anaemia. Because the symptoms are so variable and similar to other diseases, the diagnosis of the coeliac condition should always be made by a doctor.

Symptoms can appear at any age. They may first appear when a baby is weaned onto foods containing gluten, or in a few cases they may appear first in old age. Some doctors now think that weaning babies onto foods containing gluten may increase the chances of the coeliac condition arising in later life. Bread and biscuits containing wheat flour should not be introduced into the young child's diet for the first seven months. If there is any family history of adverse reactions to food then the baby's diet should be free of gluten for the first year.

When a person suffering from the coeliac condition first starts a gluten-free diet the response may be dramatic but usually a slow but steady improvement over several weeks or months can be expected. This is because of the time it takes for the lining of the digestive system to regrow.

A coeliac on a gluten-free diet should remain on this diet for life. The immune system will remember gluten and although the response to an isolated inadvertent intake of gluten may be slight, a repeated stimulation to the immune system can caused prolonged damage. This can occur with few apparent symptoms.

Vitamins

Vitamin	Major function of vitamin	Deficiency
A Retinol	Needed for light sensitive cells in the eye	Poor night vision
D Calciferol	Production of hard bones and teeth	Rickets, osteomalacia
E Tocopherol	Many functions	Sterility
K Phylloquinone	Production of blood-clotting factors	Bleeding
B_1 Thiamine	Many functions	Beri-beri
B_2 Riboflavine	Many functions	Ulceration
PP Nicotinic Acid	Many functions	Pellagra
B_5 Pantothenic acid	Many functions	Fatigue and muscle cramps
B_6 Pyridoxine	Amino acid syntheses	Many
B_{12} Cobalamin	Formation of red blood cells	Pernicious anaemia
M Folic acid	Formation of red blood cells	Anaemia
C Ascorbic acid	Many functions	Scurvy
H Biotin	Many functions	

Conversion Tables

Temperatures

gas mark	°F	°C
½	250	120
1	275	140
2	300	150
3	325	160
4	350	180
5	375	190
6	400	200
7	425	220
8	450	230
9	475	240

Weights

ounces	grams (approximate)	grams (accurate)
1	25	28
2	50	57
3	75	85
4	100	113
5	150	142
6	175	170
7	200	198
8	225	227
9	250	255
10	275	283
11	300	312
12	325	340
13	350	368
14	400	396
15	425	425
16 (1 lb)	450	454

Liquid measures

fl oz	pint	millilitres (approximate)	millilitres (accurate)
½		15	14
1		30	28
2		60	56
3		·90	85
4		125	113
5	¼	150	142
6		175	170
7		200	199
8		230	227
9		260	256
10	½	280	283
15	¾	425	425
20	1	550	567
30	1½	850	851
35	1¾	1000 (1 litre)	992

1 teaspoon = 1 level teaspoon = ½ fl oz = 5 ml

1 tablespoon = 1 level tablespoon = 1½ fl oz = 45 ml